LISTEN for *His* VOICE

HEARING GOD'S VOICE IN THE EVERYDAY OF EVERY DAY

"May the Lord keep in perfect peace those whose minds are steadfast; Because they trust in Him."
Isaiah 26:3

Marie T. Palecek

Blessings to you!

Marie T. Palecek

The website addresses suggested throughout this book are offered as a resource to you. These websites are not intended in any way to be or imply an endorsement on the part of the author and publisher, nor do we vouch for their content.

ISBN

Published by Marie T. Palecek Publishing, North Branch, Minnesota.

Team: Jennifer Kochert and Mindy Kiker of FlourishWriters, and Beth L. Dutton.

Editor: Gleniece Lytle, desertrainediting.com

Cover Design and interior formatting: Nelly Murariu at PixBeeDesign.com

Printed in the United States of America

First Edition 2022

This book is dedicated to my readers.

Ultimately, without you, these words would just be journal entries.

May each of us continue to embrace the fulfillment of God's promise in Ephesians 3:16–19 in the everyday of every day.

I pray that out of his glorious riches he may strengthen you with power through his Spirit in your inner being, so that Christ may dwell in your hearts through faith. And I pray that you, being rooted and established in love, may have power, together with all the Lord's holy people, to grasp how wide and long and high and deep is the love of Christ, and to know this love that surpasses knowledge—that you may be filled to the measure of all the fullness of God.

—Ephesians 3:16–19

Contents

Prologue

For the word of God is alive and active.
Sharper than any double-edged sword,
it penetrates even to dividing soul
and spirit, joints and marrow;
it judges the thoughts and attitudes of the heart.

—Hebrews 4:12

Have you ever longed to sit at Jesus' feet like the disciples did? Or wished God still used flaming bushes or dew-soaked fleece to confirm His will? Have you ever wondered what it would be like to stroll through the garden in the cool of the evening with the Lord God Almighty, like Adam and Eve once did? Imagine if you sat on a beach or hillside as Jesus taught using objects and events from this century. Imagine relevant stories bursting with truth and power to deepen your love and understanding of our awesome God!

If God is the same yesterday, today, and always, where are the burning bushes, talking donkeys, gentle whispers from cliffs, or magnificent pillars of fire? Yet, what if God used twenty-first century technology and shot off an email, posted on Facebook, Twitter, Instagram, or sent a text? Be honest. Would you take it seriously? Would you risk a computer virus or identity theft? Would you label it as spam?

Seriously, if God used any Old Testament drama to get our attention, would we not run the other way rather than pause to comprehend a message from our Creator? Still . . . it would be nice to have some dewy fleece once in a while.

We listen to God's voice when we read Scripture, but as we resume our busy day, those verses lay on the counter, desk, or shelf. Fortunately for us, His Word remains alive and active. When the ears of our heart remain attentive to His voice amidst the noise, God reveals Himself to us. So, how do our ears remain attentive?

We listen to a variety of things every day: music, traffic, podcasts, phone messages, conversations, birds, noise. But what do we listen for?

We listen for our BINGO numbers, our turn at the DMV, or our overdue teen to come through the door. My dog listens to me when we are together, but while I am at work, she listens for the sound of my car in the driveway.

> *Our God is amazingly creative in communicating His heart with those who have ears to hear.*

Our God is amazingly creative in communicating His heart with those who have ears to hear. Not audibly, of course. We would all freak out if that happened. God uses quiet nudges in our hearts and gentle whispers in our spirits. Sometimes He presents clarity only our hearts can hear.

Listen For His Voice is a composite of lessons, insights, convictions, challenges, and comfort my heart has heard. While some devotions contain biblical background or modern trivia, most are everyday events that transcend my simple mind's ability to comprehend and appreciate how truly awesome and loving God is.

The resounding truth is that God is the same yesterday, today, and always. He walked with Adam and Eve every day. And it is His desire to walk with you and me every day too. He longs to fill us with joy and infuse us with His love. My most sincere desire is that these devotions will motivate you to discover the joy of listening for His voice. The LISTEN section, following each devotion, is designed to assist you.

Enjoy these moments. Glean the wisdom initially revealed in simple concepts inspired by the loving and active Word of God. Open your ears that you might hear so the Lord our God can touch your heart in a way only He can.

For those who might be interested, there is also a **Listen for More** section in the back of the book. This section contains additional information as it pertains to a few devotions. You will find recipes, instructions to de-skunk your dog, and other snippets.

Introduction to the *Listen* section

Have you ever sat outside with your eyes closed and listened? At first you hear noise. Eventually, noise converts to distinct sounds: a bird, a child's laughter, a bee, the wind, the crack of a bat as it hits a ball, a distant bark. It is amazing what you hear when you listen. Yet, as your day resumes, those distinct sounds soon revert to noise.

Does your quiet time in God's Word seem to follow a similar pattern? For a few moments, God's voice is clear in His Word and within your heart. Yet, as your day resumes, that clarity seems to get absorbed in the noise.

> *We have trained ourselves to listen to His voice in the Scriptures, but we do not listen for it.*

You are not alone. We have trained ourselves to listen *to* His voice in the Scriptures, but we do not listen *for* it once we close the Book.

Some martial arts students train blindfolded and can accurately discern their opponent's position and movement. With practice, this level of awareness remains effective even when the blindfold is removed. What if we applied that same concept to Scripture? What if we increased our sensitivity and awareness so that we continued to listen *for* God's voice after our Bible was closed?

This devotional is specifically designed to encourage you towards that endeavor. Each devotion concludes with a LISTEN section as a tutorial to listen for His voice.

Psalm 1:2 says, "But they delight in the law of the Lord, meditating on it day and night" (NLT). Inspired by the guidelines in this verse, you are encouraged to pause after each devotion to meditate for at least a day and a night on what God might reveal. Use the suggestions provided, something from the devotion, or wherever God leads you.

As you LISTEN, journal what God reveals to you in the space provided or in a separate notebook. I suggest dating your journal entries. As you revisit a devotion, God will reveal fresh insights.

> Listening must
> be intentional
> before it becomes
> intuitive.

His Word is alive and active. His love and His insights are "new every morning" (Lamentations 3:23). He never changes, but He changes us.

Do not be discouraged if this feels awkward at first. Listening must be intentional before it becomes intuitive. Trust the Holy Spirit to guide you.

Even if you choose not to journal, I suggest reading through the questions. You might be surprised to hear God's whisper in your heart when you least expect it.

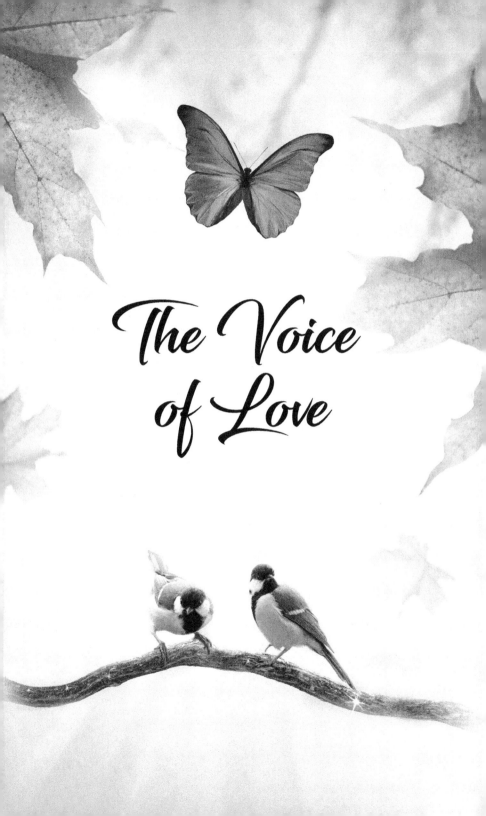

The Voice
of Love

The Shepherd's Voice

My sheep listen to my voice;
I know them, and they follow me.

—John 10:27

L ucky. Come."

"Lucky. Leave it."

"LUCKY. COME."

"I SAID COME!!!"

Lucky was in his element. His owner was not. Everyone for miles could hear the frustration, like a pot boiling over on the stove. Everyone, that is, except Lucky. Frantically, he circled the brush pile, the scent fueling his tail like a jet ready for takeoff. Crouched, safe for the moment, the rabbit twitched its nose with no intention to resurface until the enthusiastic golden lab abandoned his pursuit. A quiet small voice shattered the dramatic scene.

"Lucky isn't deaf, sir. He's ignoring you." The uninvited, unappreciated truth floated up from a group of youngsters intently constructing a sandcastle. Lucky's owner spun around towards the small voice, ready to pounce upon the innocent but honest proclamation. Yet the offender lacked the common courtesy to even look up from his creation.

"What do you know?" he growled at the huddled group of architects.

"No offense, sir," came the brave reply. "You keep raising your voice, but Lucky just isn't listening. That rabbit is calling his name." With a disarming smile, the red-haired, freckled-faced boy's gentle wisdom defused the anger Lucky's owner directed toward his dog's defiance.

A cheerful, "Lucky! Wanna go bye-bye?" instantly nullified the rabbit's appeal as Lucky bounded toward his master, eager for their next adventure.

He was lucky to have Lucky. He knew that. They found each other shortly after he accepted Jesus as his Lord and Savior. However, an abusive childhood, failed marriage, plus a series of poor choices hindered his ability to accept God's unconditional love. Until Lucky.

Have you accepted Jesus as Lord and Savior, yet still feel His unconditional love must be earned? Does the thought of His unconditional love feel like you are setting yourself up to be disappointed? Does remorse over past mistakes strangle your ability to accept God's unconditional love unconditionally?

Lucky was his mentor and friend. Lucky's love was tangible. It was real. Lucky listened for the truck's engine and with unrestrained jubilance, greeted his master whether he had been gone all day or just a few moments. They navigated life together with long walks and heartfelt talks. If Lucky's love was unconditional, could God's love could be unconditional too?

The warm afternoon sun ignited a chorus of feathered friends to chase away the morning's chill. Softly, an impression entered the man's heart. "I am the Good Shepherd," it whispered. "I know my sheep and my sheep know me. They listen to my voice." He recognized the words of Jesus from John's Gospel (John chapter 10). The thought settled in his heart like a fog, and followed him on their stroll like an unexpected entity. The strange thing was, it did not seem strange at all.

"Follow the Good Shepherd." The entity whispered, "Listen to His voice."

"Follow me," Jesus says over twenty time in the Gospels.

"My sheep listen to my voice; I know them, and they follow me" (John 10:27).

Within a secret place, his heart opened with an overwhelming desire to be still and know God (Psalm 46:10). Let that truth sink in. There was no doubt Lucky had heard him, but like the kid said, the rabbit was calling his name. The sheep of the Good Shepherd listen to His voice and follow willingly.

As their walk continued, Lucky's master sensed the Shepherd's loving voice speak directly to his heart. It seemed as natural as it was bizarrely unnatural. Yet he listened.

> *Lucky's master sensed the Shepherd's loving voice speak directly to his heart.*

In biblical times, shepherds would often gather several flocks in the safety of a sheep pen or cave for the night. In the morning, intermingled flocks listened for their shepherd's voice and followed him to green pastures (John 10:3–4). How did they recognize their shepherd's voice?

During their days grazing on quiet hillsides, sheep listened *to* their shepherd's voice so that it was familiar and comforting. In the chaos of the sheep pen, sheep listened *for* their trusted shepherd's voice and obediently followed despite the interesting conversations about the other sheep's adventures.

By nature, dogs study their masters and instinctively learn their routine. Lucky knows whether his master is getting up for a sandwich, going for a walk, or out the door to work. He offers his favorite toy whenever his master feels down. With adamant devotion, he clearly communicates that any moment spent with his beloved master is an eternity of joy.

Normally, Lucky gladly obeys the slightest hint of a command. But rabbits are his downfall. And squirrels. He simply cannot resist when they call his name. During his long days on the couch, even with the radio on, there is only one sound his ears listen for—the sound of his master's truck. Oh, what joy fills his heart as it pulls into the driveway. When the door finally opens, and he hears, "Hello, dear friend, did you miss me?" his jubilance overflows.

> *If the Lord is my shepherd, my Good Shepherd, who loves me unconditionally, what kind of sheep am I?*

Under a sprawling oak, their favorite bench invites Lucky's master to contemplate the Shepherd's words. A pair of mated trumpeter swans gracefully ripple the glass-smooth surface of the quiet lake. Without warning, a thought grips him, "If the Lord is my shepherd, my Good Shepherd, who loves me unconditionally, what kind of sheep am I?"

It is imperative that sheep train their ears to listen to the shepherd's voice so that in the sheep pen they are not led astray. The morning's chaos does not permit the luxury of listening *to* the shepherd's voice with other shepherds calling and sheep *baaing* their opinions. They must listen *for* the voice they trust and willingly obey.

Lucky's master thought to himself, "Do I know my Shepherd's voice so I can hear Him calling me in the sheep pen with rabbits, squirrels, and other Baa-Hummers? Or will I listen to voices calling out *buy this, you deserve it, don't let them get away with that, everyone is doing it, it's not your fault, no one will know, it is just this one time.*

If I do not listen *to* his voice, how can I listen *for* it? Why does spending time in prayer or studying His Word feel like a chore instead of unrestrained joy? Is He my Good Shepherd or not?"

> *If I do not listen to his voice, how can I listen for it?*

The questions unnerved him. They demanded answers. Lucky pressed against his master's leg, unable to stop the tears that streamed down his master's face nor understand the emotions behind them.

"Yes, Lord," his heart spoke out loud, "Your servant is listening. I want to know You more. Fill me with a desire and thirst for Your Word. Reward my time with You so I can hear Your truth when all the world's Baa-Hummers are calling my name. Lord, I need a deeper level of devotion to listen *for* Your voice and the courage to obey. I want the depth of devotion towards You that Lucky zealously gives to me. Search me, O Lord and know my heart. Fill me with joy in Your presence" (His prayer was inspired by 1 Samuel 3:9; Psalms 139:23; Acts 2:28). Gratefully, he wrapped his arms around Lucky and felt the warm embrace of his Shepherd as he listened *for* His voice.

Listen

Read John 10:27

Jesus is your Good Shepherd. He knows you. He knows the Baa-Hummers that call your name. We need to listen *to* His voice in our quiet time so that we can listen *for* His voice in the busyness of each day.

† List a few Baa-Hummers that distract you or try to lead you astray.

† How can a good sheep hear the Good Shepherd's voice over the noise?

† Do you intentionally listen *to* His voice? What hinders you from listening *for* it?

† Journal how the Good Shepherd ministered to you this day and night.

LISTEN FOR HIS VOICE

Fifth-Sparrow Status

Are not two sparrows sold for a penny?
Yet not one of them will fall to the
ground outside your Father's care.

—Matthew 10:29

Are not five sparrows sold for two pennies?
Yet not one of them is forgotten by God.
Indeed, the very hairs of your head are all numbered.
Don't be afraid; you are worth more
than many sparrows.

—Luke 12:6–7

After nine years of infertility tests and procedures, Abby and Paul finally conceived. When their son was born, Abby returned to work with some misgivings. When miracle number two came along, Abby decided to invest her time and energy at home raising her children. While she relished her time at home, a monthly luncheon of adult conversation with former co-workers satisfied her itch to stay connected.

"What is wrong?" Paul asked after one such outing. "You seem so down. Did something happen at lunch today?"

Abby struggled to put feelings into words. She shared how her former co-workers asked how she could give up such a vital role in the company "just" to be a mom. It hurt. She absolutely loved being a full-time mom but was also fully aware of the exciting life she left behind. She was frustrated and confused as to how to respond. Her wise husband hugged her close and whispered in her ear, "Honey, next time they ask how you could walk away from such a fulfilling career, tell them it is okay. Tell them you just got a promotion."

> *Too often we value how others e-VALUE-ate us regardless of what we know to be true.*

Despite our best efforts, too often we value how others e-VALUE-ate us regardless of what we know to be true. This is not limited to people. We feel validated by our heavenly Father when He answers our prayers with abundant blessings. This gives us confidence and crowds out fear and doubt. We feel His great love for us affirmed through His blessings.

Yet, other times God seems silent as we wade through waist-high, shoe sucking muck, while Satan's taunts ring with a microscopic ounce of truth. We are overwhelmed and feel abandoned, lost, and alone. How can we feel valued when we're at our lowest low? What good is it to remember God is the same yesterday, today, and always when today we cannot feel His love?

Jesus addressed this concern in Matthew 6:26, "Look at the birds. They don't plant or harvest or store food in barns, for your heavenly Father feeds them. And aren't you far more valuable to him than they are?" (NLT).

Have you ever wondered how much a bird is worth? Both Matthew and Luke referred to the monetary value of sparrows. "Are not two sparrows sold for a penny?" (Mathew 10:29). "Are not five sparrows sold for two pennies? . . . Don't be afraid; you are worth more than many sparrows" (Luke 12:6–7).

Jesus reveals the sparrow's value to reassure us how much more our heavenly Father values us. Of course, being told you are worth more than a flock of sparrows would hardly be considered a compliment. Maybe a dozen bald eagles or a flock of trumpeter swans, but sparrows? Not so much.

Specialty shops cater to bird lovers of all ages with bird feeders and birdseed specifically designed for cardinals or thistle feeders to attract finches. There are suet feeders for nuthatches and downy woodpeckers. In addition, there are a variety of oriole and hummingbird feeders to satisfy the most avid bird watcher. Shelves are crammed with books devoted to bluebirds, wood ducks, grosbeak, and other feathered friends. The available products identify which species we value most.

There is no special birdseed for sparrows. No uniquely designed sparrow houses. No books designated for sparrows. You can find, however, chapters devoted to minimizing your sparrow population.

Sparrows are worthless, unappreciated feathered guests. Yet God has taken care of their needs. He created them to be resourceful, cheerful, and generous. Sparrows are usually the first to discover when you've refilled the feeder and quickly spread the news with cheerful chirps that say, "Thanks, human," and then announce to the bird world, "Hey guys. Look. Fresh food."

> *What good is it to remember God is the same yesterday, today, and always when today you cannot feel His love?*

Sparrows are resilient and refuse to fly south when winter approaches. God gave them a cheerful song that rings through the winter air to spread warmth on the coldest day. God provides them with food, shelter, and companionship. Their hollow bones are strong and their eyes sharp and alert. The soft, downy brood feathers provide a warm and comfortable nest lining. Their survival is not dependent upon their status at the feeder, on the bookshelf, or in the minds of bird enthusiasts, but upon a God who loves them and provides all their needs.

It is hard to imagine a lower status than a sparrow. However Scripture reveals it in the two verses quoted above. Did you catch it? Here they are again: "Are not two sparrows sold for a penny?" and "Are not five sparrows sold for two pennies?" Two sparrows were sold for an *assarion*, the smallest Roman coin made of copper, thus translated as a penny. Five sparrows were worth two assarions. The fifth sparrow was thrown in for free, meaning it had virtually no value to either buyer or seller. It was most likely a runt, a cripple, or one that was just too old to sell at full price (which was half a penny). Yet, Jesus assures us that our heavenly Father is keenly aware of each tuft of feather, each tiny beat of its heart, and each whisper of breath.

> *Have you felt like that fifth sparrow?*

Have you felt like that fifth sparrow? Has someone made you feel like you are just a mom? Or just a clerk? Or just a stepparent? Or just another retiree? Satan taunted Job about his fifth-sparrow status. Job's wife berated him when she said, "Are you still maintaining your integrity? Curse God and die!" (Job chapters 1 and 2). Simon Peter felt it on the beach when Jesus asked him for the third time, "Simon, do you love me?" (John chapter 21). The widow who placed two copper coins in the temple treasury was fifth-sparrow status, yet Jesus said of her, "Truly I tell you, this poor widow has put in more than all the others" (Luke 21:3).

Naturally, we would rather embrace God's love manifested in blessings and prosperity. Trusting in the Lord is easier when things are going well, when the answer to prayer meets our expectations, and life is good. Not much faith is required when life is bountiful and filled with good fortune.

However, with fifth-sparrow status, our faith and trust are totally dependent on our knowledge and relationship with our Almighty God. As a fifth sparrow, we must remember whose we are, not who we are.

We prefer to avoid fifth-sparrow status, yet during our lowest of lows our comprehension of God's love and grandeur is revealed in how He values us. God is God. It is as simple as that. He is God when we praise Him from the mountaintop. He is the same God when our feet are stuck in muck, and we have nothing to give Him except our cries for help.

> *As a fifth sparrow, we must remember whose we are, not who we are.*

Our Lord is the Creator of the universe. He clothes the mountains with majesty and awe. He guides the butterfly's delicate wings. He strengthens the grizzly's powerful grip. He feels the sparrow's fragile heartbeat. Each creature is under the ever watchful, caring, loving eye of the Father. Rest in the assurance that our value is not dependent upon who we are—but *whose* we are. Even when we feel the sting of fifth-sparrow status, we need to remember God is God, and we are His. That is the only status that is valid.

Listen

Read Mathew 10:29 and Luke 12:6

Invest a few minutes listening to birds. If you do not have access to a live concert, search "birds singing" via YouTube or iTunes or an app of nature sounds. Invite God to speak to your soul while you listen.

† When have you felt like a fifth sparrow—worthless, unappreciated, or unwanted?

† As your day resumes, be aware of other "sparrows" in your flock.

† Look for an opportunity to minister to a fellow sparrow.

† Journal what you learned this day and night that only a fifth sparrow can understand about God.

Limburger Cheese Theology

Don't be quick to fly off the handle. Anger boomerangs.
You can spot a fool by the lumps on his head.

—Ecclesiastes 7:9 (MSG)

L ife comes with personalized irritations. While we handle some annoyances better than others, we all have something that ignites our short fuse. On any particular day, it could be a careless driver, an aimless shopper, a spilled glass of milk, or a lost cell phone. When these moments come in quick succession, and you start to believe the whole world really does stink, maybe Grandpa Kent and this Limburger cheese theology can help turn things around.

Grandpa Kent was a loveable, old farmer with a grumpy demeanor. He adored his grandkids but lacked the skills and patience a full day's visit required. The constant activity, energy, and noise soon drained his tolerance. By noon his stamina was exhausted. Despite the hard outer shell, Grandpa Kent's deep affection for his grandkids challenged him to keep his temper in check. His best defense was an escape for a long afternoon nap, which refreshed his spirit enough that he was only mildly grumpy the remainder of their visit. The grandkids were as delighted with the gently grumpy side of their beloved grandpa as they were with Grandma's famous chocolate chip cookies.

One afternoon, as he laid down for his nap, the grandkids got a mischievous, although not so bright, idea. As Grandpa Kent snored, they carefully smeared some Limburger cheese on his trademark handlebar mustache. As a rumbling snore brought the aroma up his nose, Grandpa Kent woke up early from his nap, which was never a good thing.

He sat up and said, "Boy. Something sure stinks in here."

As he went into the hall, he sniffed. "Man, it stinks out here too."

He went downstairs into the kitchen and took a big whiff. "My goodness, Ma," he said, "I don't know what you are cooking, but it sure stinks."

He walked into the parlor. "It stinks in here too," he thought. "This whole house stinks. How long has it been since Ma did any real cleaning? I gotta get me some fresh air."

> *Oh, my word. The whole world stinks!*

Grandpa Kent stepped out onto the porch and took a big whiff of Limburger cheese. "Oh, my word. The whole world stinks!"

Life has its own Limburger moments: those things that can make your world stink. Despite your best efforts, you cannot avoid Limburger cheese. People can be irritating, unreasonable, and just plain difficult. Tires go flat, computers crash, refrigerators quit without warning, and some people wear flip-flops that go "flap-flap-flap-splat."

Our human nature complicates the situation. Maybe you are not a morning person or have a short fuse for waiting in line. Maybe you left a little later than expected, and traffic was heavier than normal. We might, like Grandpa Kent, have a low tolerance for kids. If we are not careful, life's Limburger cheese will begin to influence our thoughts until we start to believe our life really does stink.

Even when we try to get a breath of fresh air to clear our thoughts, Limburger cheese is right there, spoiling our view. There is enough Limburger cheese in our lives to agree with Grandpa Kent. Yes, some things in this world stink. But we do not have to allow them to steal our joy and our peace. We have choices.

Life viewed through Limburger vapors is only one option. We have intellect. Sometimes, like Grandpa Kent, we ignore what we know to be true. He knew Ma was a great cook and kept

> *We place unreasonable expectations on each other and then justify our anger when people fail to measure up.*

the house in order, yet he let Limburger cloud his judgment and contaminate his words.

We have Limburger emotions, especially anger, and find ourselves saying things like, "He/she only does that to irritate me." You are angry. Of course, you are. Who wouldn't be? Limburger cheese always justifies anger.

You had a tough day at work. You are tired. You have not been able to vent all day. You expect compassion and support when you walk through the door at home, but the ones you depend on for empathy had a challenging day too. It does not matter what sparks the explosion: it is never your fault, right? "If he didn't . . ." "If she would only . . ." We place unreasonable expectations on each other and then justify our anger when people fail to measure up. Do not blame each other. Blame Limburger cheese.

Projects fail. Dogs throw up on the carpet. Bosses have unreasonable expectations. Toilets get clogged. Cars drift into your lane. The vapors have been building up all day, so the tiniest spark sets off the explosion, and Limburger stink is everywhere.

Grandpa Kent allowed Limburger cheese to cloud his judgment. When the only common denominator in conflicts with your spouse, kids, clerks, co-workers, or crazy drivers is *you*, maybe it is Limburger-cheese mentality. Are you going to trust Limburger cheese or give the benefit of doubt even when there is a whiff of Limburger in the air?

One young mother found herself constantly angry at her children for one thing or another. "I have two great kids," she admitted. "I hated being angry all the time. I decided to limit myself to ten outbursts a day and work my way towards zero. It really helped. But honestly, sometimes I used up a whole day's quota by 9 a.m."

We must refuse to live under the influence of Limburger cheese. Wash it off. Let the love of Christ wash over you in such a way that your actions will reflect God's love like a refreshing spring rain. Jesus showed the disciples the full extent of His love by washing their feet. He even washed Judas's feet. Then He commanded them to wash one another's feet (John 13:14). Let God's love wash over you, cleansing the Limburger effects so you can extend His love even when it seems like the whole world stinks. Prepare to be amazed as you become aware of how much God blesses you in the process.

Did you know there was Limburger cheese at the last supper? In Luke chapter 22, Jesus served the bread and wine, then announced Judas's betrayal. The disciples "ask[ed] each other which of them would ever do such a thing. Then they began to argue among themselves about who would be the greatest among them" (Luke 22:23–24). Even Jesus had to deal with squabbles at the dinner table. Notice how Jesus handled it. He gently reminded them that "I am among you as one who serves" (Luke 22:27). How quickly they forget that He had just washed their feet.

When Limburger anger and frustration threaten to dominate your next reaction, do what Jesus did: do something for the other person. Jesus washed their feet. Of course, that might not be an option for you.

We cannot always control how we feel in a Limburger moment, but we can control how we react. Stuck in Limburger traffic? Slow down. Smile. Purposely breathe with your stomach muscles. Allow another driver to "be stupid" without Limburger criticism.

Are you in a Limburger checkout line with someone who cannot count to fifteen? Did the new clerk just page the supervisor? Again? Take a deep breath, smile, compliment someone to neutralize the vapors.

Got Limburger kids? Smile. Take a snack break or bake some cookies. Have a spontaneous race or a how-high-can-you-jump contest. Tell them you can jump higher than a house (this will only work once). Let them show you how high they can jump. Smile as their energy chases away Limburger fumes. When it is your turn, jump and say, "Houses cannot jump." Limburger be gone.

Do you have a Limburger spouse? Smile. Express genuine gratitude for something specific or compliment them. Give a hug. Invite them to sit down to relax. Take a walk to talk about their day. Wash their feet or tell them you can jump higher than a house. Defuse Limburger vapers with acts of kindness.

Limburger moments are opportunities for us to extend God's unconditional love and forgiveness for the Limburger moments we inflict on others. Let Limburger cheese theology provide opportunities to practice God's grace. After washing their feet, Jesus promised His disciples that they would be blessed whenever they did as He had done (John 13:17). God rewards our obedience, especially in the nasty moments that

> *Limburger moments are opportunities for us to extend God's unconditional love and forgiveness for the Limburger moments we inflict on others.*

stink up our lives. When we do as Jesus did—serve others—
it converts Limburger moments into blessings.

Here are a few Limburger antidotes:
Take one or more daily as needed.

Rejoice in the Lord always. I will say it again: Rejoice! Let
your gentleness be evident to all. The Lord is near. Do not be
anxious about anything, but in every situation, by prayer
and petition, with thanksgiving, present your requests to God.
And the peace of God, which transcends all understanding,
will guard your hearts and your minds in Christ Jesus.

—Philippians 4:4–7

Let the word of Christ dwell in you richly in all wisdom,
teaching and admonishing one another in psalms and
hymns and spiritual songs, singing with grace in your
hearts to the Lord.

—Colossians 3:16 (NKJV)

Be thankful in all circumstances.

—1 Thessalonians 5:18

But the fruit of the Spirit is love, joy, peace, forbearance, kindness, goodness, faithfulness, gentleness and self-control.
Against such things there is no law.

—Galatians 5:22–23

Be kind and compassionate to one another, forgiving each other, just as in Christ God forgave you.

—Ephesians 4:32

I can do all things through Christ who strengthens me.

—Philippians 4:13 (NKJV)

Sensible people control their temper; they earn respect by overlooking wrongs.

—Proverbs 19:11 (NLT)

Don't grumble against one another, brothers and sisters, or you will be judged. The Judge is standing at the door!

—James 5:9

The eyes of the Lord search the whole earth in order to strengthen those whose hearts are fully committed to him.

—2 Chronicles 16:9 (NLT)

Never pay back evil with more evil. Do things in such a way that everyone can see you are honorable. Do all that you can to live in peace with everyone.

—Romans 12:17–18 (NLT)

Listen

Read Ephesians 4:32

You cannot control Limburger moments. But you can control your response. Be kind and considerate. Have an attitude of gratitude. Limburger cannot coexist with gratitude. In a world that stinks, be a breath of fresh air. As Grandpa Kent might say, "Get rid of that stinkin' thinkin'."

† Find an antidote for the Limburger on your pet-peeves list.

† Put some Limburger antidotes in your pocket to apply whenever your handlebar mustache twitches today.

† How effective were your Limburger antidotes?

† Journal your Limburger moments and blessings this day and night.

LISTEN FOR HIS VOICE

When God Ruins Everything

Yet you, Lord, are our Father.
We are the clay, you are the potter;
we are all the work of your hand.

—Isaiah 64:8

T his stupid stuff. It won't do anything. I can't even make spaghetti. It's no use." With a thunderous thud, the glob of Play-Doh® slammed onto the innocent table.

"I quit," he announced with crossed arms while his foot registered its vote on the matter.

It did not require much detective work to discern the source of my son's frustration. The much-loved glob of dough was too dry to form a ball or go through the press. My first thought was, *That's life. Get used to it.* Thankfully, the words never spilled out. With hands still wet from washing dishes, I quickly grabbed the uncooperative glob of dough and massaged it.

"No." he wailed as the tears began to flow. "No, Mom, no! You're gonna ruin everything." Any attempt to explain would have been as futile as offering comfort. Besides, it would all be over in a matter of seconds. Victoriously, I plopped the restored glob down on the table in front of my astonished son who realized I had not ruined everything. Mom had fixed it!

With peace and the dough restored, my son contentedly resumed his Play-Doh® creations, and I resumed my task at the sink.

Have you ever experienced times in life when you just wanted to cross your arms and cry, "I quit!"? Have you ever wished life's unyielding problems could be fixed as easily as my wet hands fixed the dried-out Play-Doh®? I have. If only God would just take the glob of my life in His hands and gently restore what was not working.

I was frustrated with life. Things were not like I had planned. I wanted to quit, to throw in the towel like my son threw down the glob of dry dough. It seemed the harder I tried, the worse things got. Why was God so resistant to answering my prayers?

Something stirred within my attitude, awakened by the memory of the dough in my hands. "I am the potter; you are the clay." The words drifted into my heart like a whisper. Its warmth tingled through me like a soothing electrical current. Yet, "I am the potter; you are the clay," did not feel like the answer I sought.

If only God would just take the glob of my life in His hands and gently restore what was not working.

My fingers remembered how the hard, dry lump of dough felt in my hands. At first, it resisted the water as my fingers pushed and kneaded. Finally, it was flexible, ready to be put back into service. Was my spirit dry and unyielding and resistant to change? Did my spirit scream at God, "You're gonna ruin everything"?

As if it were real, I felt cold water splash in my face. I struggled and wiggled with all my might. But the potter gently worked my clay heart with His wet hands. "I am the potter; you are the clay," echoed within my heart until I felt myself yield to His gentle but firm touch.

My cracks became supple. The hard shell softened as His loving caress drove the resistance from my soul. Everything was different, although nothing had changed—except the Potter's hands on the clay.

He gently massages living water into dry resistant clay until we yield to, then yearn for, His touch.

When God ruins everything with His wet hands, He gently massages living water into dry resistant clay until we yield to, then yearn for, His touch. "Yet you, Lord, are our Father. We are the clay; you are the potter; we are all the work of your hand" (Isaiah 64:8).

Listen

Read Isaiah 64:8

Take a glob of Play-Doh® in your hands. Close your eyes and massage it for a while. Focus on how the clay feels. Then mold it into a bowl or vase to represent your life in God's hands. I included two recipes for homemade clay in **Listen for More**, pages 225-226.

† Where is your glob of clay right now? In the Potter's hands? Going through the press? Plopped on a shelf? Buried beneath debris? Lost?

† What is the condition of your clay? Yielding? Resisting? Dry and cracked? Restored? Hard or broken? Flexible? Confused?

† As your day resumes, feel the Potter's hands. Listen for His voice.

† Let your "glob of clay" journal what God revealed this day and night. How did the Potter's hands feel? How did your clay respond? Did the water refresh or sting?

LISTEN FOR HIS VOICE

Lord, I Need to be Kneaded

Knead me, Lord, with firm and gentle hands.
Mold me according to Your master plan.
Even those events that seem so mundane
Are kneaded along with the joy and pain.

I need to be kneaded with loving care.
The yeast of Your Spirit blended with prayer.
Punch my self-inflated ego down.
Let no pride or malice in me be found.

And please knead out any resistance
So I can rise above every circumstance.
Then cover me with Your cloak of grace.
Draw me nearer in Your warm embrace.

Provide protection from drafts that chill.
That threaten to lead me against Your will.
Remind me, however busy life gets,
I need time in Your Word and time to rest.

Knead me, Lord, so the aroma of my life
Will be to You a pleasing sacrifice.
Dear Lord, until my life is completed
I know I will always need to be kneaded.

What Needs to be Kneaded in Your Life Today?

> So Abraham ran back to the tent and said to Sarah, "Hurry! Get three large measures of your best flour, knead it into dough, and bake some bread."
>
> —Genesis 18:6 (NLT)

Basic bread combines six simple ingredients: flour, water, yeast, sugar, salt, and oil. Unlike cakes which are mixed then baked, bread requires several stages, each with a unique purpose. During the process, the dough needs to be kneaded several times before it is ready for the oven. Between the kneading, it needs to rest, rise, be covered, protected, and punched down.

What needs to be kneaded in your life today? In John 6:48, Jesus says, "I am the bread of life." He is able to knead what is needed whether it is rest, comfort, protection, conviction, or guidance. Let one or more of these verses speak to the "knead" in your heart today:

> For the bread of God is the bread that comes down from heaven and gives life to the world.
>
> —John 6:33

> Then Jesus declared, "I am the bread of life. Whoever comes to me will never go hungry, and whoever believes in me will never be thirsty."
>
> —John 6:35

> Jesus answered, "It is written: 'Man shall not live on bread alone, but on every word that comes from the mouth of God.'"
>
> —Matthew 4:4

He will cover you with his feathers, and under his wings you will find refuge; his faithfulness will be your shield and rampart.

—Psalm 91:4

For we are to God the pleasing aroma of Christ among those who are being saved and those who are perishing.

—2 Corinthians 2:15

Read John 6:33

Making bread is an art. To get a better understanding, watch a YouTube video on making bread or read the "Easy, Basic Home-Baked Bread" recipe in **Listen for More**, page 227. Choose one or two verses from "What Needs to be Kneaded in Your Life Today?" listed above.

✝ What does God's touch feel like? What does His voice sound like? Can you smell His essence? Can you taste His warmth?

✝ How does your dough respond to His kneading? Is it resistant or resilient? Does it feel protected or exposed? Is it active or at rest? Is your dough rising or feel punched down?

✝ Journal the insights God has revealed to you this day and night as a letter from God as He kneads the needs in your life. Invite Him to guide your pen.

LISTEN FOR HIS VOICE

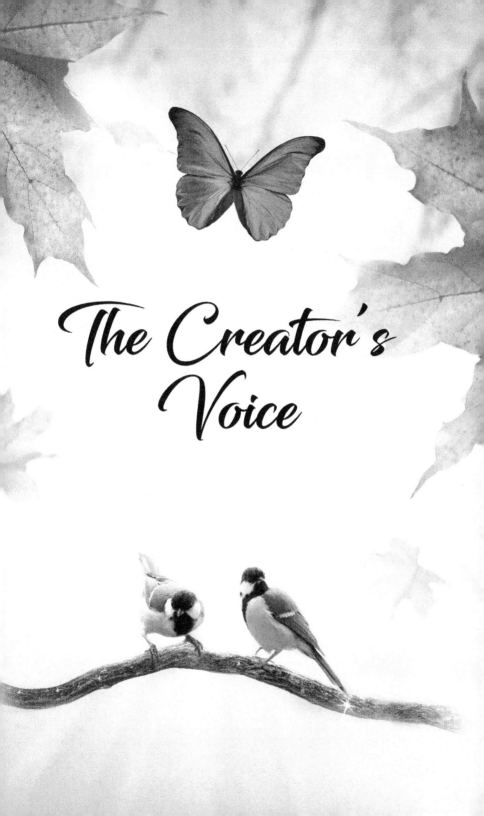

The Creator's Voice

Imagine

No eye has seen, no ear has heard, and no mind has imagined
what God has prepared for those who love him.

—1 Corinthians 2:9 (NLT)

Imagination: "The act or power of forming a mental image of something not present to the senses or never before wholly perceived in reality."[1]

When Thomas Edison imagined lighting up a room with the flip of a switch in 1879, it was *never before wholly perceived in reality*. People were in awe when his idea actually worked. Today, the only time we stand in awe is when we flip the switch—and nothing happens.

We have come to expect our phone to take photos, spellcheck, learn our lingo, send messages, share pictures, display emojis to express our mood, enable conference calling, assist with navigation, surf the internet, pay bills, deposit checks, and find the nearest restaurant in the cuisine of our current craving. We fail to consider that in 1875 Alexander Graham Bell imagined *a mental image of something not present to the senses. Something never wholly perceived in reality*, which resulted in the phone.

Time has awarded us the privilege to presume a familiarity

With our daily saturation of technology, is it any wonder we fail to value imagination?

with the lightbulb and phone, so the awe of something *never wholly perceived in reality* has lost its glamour. We stand in awe about the next generation phone or high-tech lightbulb without a thought about the men who imagined the reality we now consider mundane. With our daily saturation of technology, is it any wonder we fail to value imagination?

We know Thomas Edison and Alexander Graham Bell existed. For them to masterfully design something never perceived before testifies to their incredible minds. Is there any irrefutable evidence God is real and not just a figment of our imagination, like a *mental image of something not present to the senses and never wholly perceived in reality?*

Does God exist only to those who believe in Him? Or do they believe in Him because He exists? After all, how can we know without a doubt that someone *never wholly perceived in our reality* is really real? Romans 1:20 boldly disputes any theory of an imaginary God, saying, "For since the creation of the world God's invisible qualities—his eternal power and divine nature—have been clearly seen, being understood from what has been made, so that people are without excuse."

> *Since the beginning, nature has declared how truly awesome God is.*

Is our belief in an unseen God a stretch of our imagination or is there irrefutable proof? Is it possible to know and understand the Lord of creation, whose presence cannot be perceived in reality?

Since the beginning, nature has declared how truly awesome God is. Yet, while evidence surrounds us each day, few people pause long enough to consider the precision, the workmanship, that He crafted into fragile temporal things. For now, let's consider the honeycomb.

The honeycomb is the main infrastructure of the honeybee's hive. Without knowledge of science or mathematics, honeybees naturally design the perfect architectural structure. Hexagons provide the only geometric shape to encompass maximum storage space. They create the strongest possible construction, using the minimum amount of materials. In this case, beeswax. Since eight ounces of honey is required to produce one ounce of wax, the hexagon is a wise economical solution.

There are only two purposes of the honeycomb: store honey and incubate hatchlings. Regardless of the hive's location, each honeycomb column must be set precisely at a 13-degree angle to level ground. This prevents the honey from flowing out yet allows new hatchlings to emerge with ease.

> *God created the simple honeybee to execute with perfection a structure human engineers cannot improve upon.*

As incredible as that is, consider this: honeybees construct the honeycomb in total darkness, which protects the hive from fluctuating temperatures that exist in lighted sites. Dozens of worker bees start forming clusters of hexagons on each of the four corners, completing the outer edges first, then working toward the center. Yet, the finished product features perfectly even rows of the classic hexagonal design. If you ever attempted tiling a floor, you can more fully appreciate that kind of precision.

Incredibly, God created the simple honeybee to execute with perfection a structure human engineers cannot improve upon. If the honeycomb is something we can see and touch, imagine what Paul refers to in 1 Corinthians 2:9 when he wrote, "No eye has seen, no ear has heard, and no mind has imagined what God has prepared for those who love him" (NLT).

How often do we pause to think of Edison or Bell when we reach for our phone or flip the light switch? Do we pause to marvel at a bee's ability to create the honeycomb, let alone consider who created the bee with the ability to construct the honeycomb? Who is more AWE-mazing: the honeybee or the one who created it? Each day, we encounter intricate wonders far exceeding what we could ask for or imagine, without ever considering the One who created our world and everything in it.

Imagine for a moment the precision with which God not only prepares work for us but prepares us for the work, here on earth and especially in heaven. As we consider the work of His hands, we can rejoice with Paul's words in Ephesians 3:20. "Now to him who is able to do immeasurably more than all we ask or imagine, according to his power that is at work within us."

God expects us to enjoy what He created. He created the detailed perfection of the honeycomb for our enjoyment—not our worship. Science continually unfolds details *never wholly perceived in reality* as undeniable evidence of a Master Creator. Our awe in His creation should never surpass our awe for the Creator.

> *God not only prepares work for us but prepares us for the work.*

So, flip that light switch. Grab your phone. Taste the sweet honeycomb. Embrace a refreshing walk in the woods. Listen to the birds. Feast your eyes on the beauty of nature. Admire a delicate spider's web. Relish a glorious sunset. Rejoice in all the marvelous wonders here on earth. But never let them replace the worship that is God's and God's alone.

Reverence for the Lord is pure, lasting forever.
The laws of the Lord are true; each one is fair.
They are more desirable than gold, even the finest gold.
They are sweeter than honey, even honey dripping
from the comb.

—Psalm 19:9–10 (NLT)

Listen

Read Romans 1:20

Contemplate the masterful complexity of a honeycomb or any aspect of nature (spider web, oriole's nest, bird, feather, tree, cucumber, flower, rock, cloud, butterfly, dragonfly, toad).

† Executing a Google search is another avenue for contemplation. For honeybees, try Honey Bee Suite: A Better Way to Bee.[2]

† What does nature reveal about God's character? His love? His power?

† As your day resumes, be aware of God's presence, guidance, creativity, and providence.

† Journal what God has revealed to you about Himself this day and night.

LISTEN FOR HIS VOICE

The Potter's Kiln

And surely I am with you always,
to the very end of the age.

—Matthew 28:20

Since the late 1800s, Redwing, Minnesota has been renowned for Redwing shoes and pottery. On a recent visit, I chatted with a skilled potter while he molded a lump of clay. He renewed my appreciation for the craft and provided a new perspective on life in God's hands.

Before the potter's skillful hands place the clay on the wheel, the unique shape and purpose of the finished piece has been decided. With a few primitive tools and the spin of the wheel, the potter molds and shapes the pitcher, bowl, plate, or other item. Once formed, an image, like a leaf or flower, can be imprinted into the damp clay. If desired, color can also be added.

Only when satisfied with the creation, does the potter stamp their name into the clay. Each piece of pottery throughout the store bears the signature of the potter who created it.

Molded and stamped pottery looks finished, but unless it endures the kiln, it remains incomplete. If the potter chose to put a clay vase on a shelf, it would eventually harden as the water evaporated, but it would never be useful. Any contact with water, and the molded vase would return to a muddy lump of clay. There is only one way to prevent that: the kiln.

The kiln is a large oven hosting a temperature between 1745°F and 2455°F. The correct temperature range for a specific piece of pottery depends on the particles in the clay and the porous properties of the finished piece. A mid-range kiln is kept between 2124°F and 2264°F. A high-fire kiln is maintained between 2305°F and 2455°F. The extreme temperature of the kiln removes every drop of moisture from the pottery, but it does more than just that. The kiln completes the work the potter's hands began. Once the moisture is removed, the heat welds the clay particles together, strengthening the pottery as it produces a protective finish. Only then can it fulfill its original purpose.

It takes about twelve to fourteen hours to cure pottery. During this time, the kiln must be faithfully monitored. If the temperature gets too high or drops too low, the pottery could be ruined. Potters love their craft, but no matter how precious the vase or bowl, the potter knows it must be surrendered to the kiln.

> *The potter allows the beloved clay vessel to endure the fire of the kiln so it will be strong, useful, and fulfill its purpose.*

The piece of pottery leaves the potter's hand, but is never out of their watchful, protective eye. The potter never leaves their precious creation at the mercy of the kiln. Faithfully, the process is monitored to ensure the end product becomes the envisioned masterpiece. From the moment the potter's hands first grasp the wet clay, the potter safeguards each piece from the wheel all the way through the fiery furnace, never allowing the kiln to ruin what took so long to accomplish.

The potter allows the beloved clay vessel to endure the fire of the kiln so it will be strong, useful, and fulfill its purpose. God allowed Joseph to endure the kiln of his brothers' jealousy, the accusations of Potiphar's wife, and Pharaoh's prison so he could accomplish God's purpose (Genesis chapters 37–50). Job endured his own kiln, but triumphed.

Our heavenly Potter is faithful and steadfast. But nowhere in Scripture is it written that God so loved the world that He protected his clay from adversity. Instead, over and over, God assures us:

✝ "Have I not commanded you? Be strong and courageous. Do not be afraid; do not be discouraged, for the Lord your God will be with you wherever you go" (Joshua 1:9).

✝ "Even though I walk through the darkest valley, I will fear no evil, for you are with me; your rod and your staff, they comfort me" (Psalm 23:4).

✝ "In this world you will have trouble. But take heart! I have overcome the world" (John 16:33).

✝ Jesus' last words in Matthew's Gospel were "And surely I am with you always, to the very end of the age" (Matthew 28:20).

Why do we need so much reassurance? Because we will encounter troubles, trials, enemies, and hardships. We may even feel desolate. But rest assured, we are not abandoned.

The potter carefully prepares the clay, so it has everything it needs to fulfill its purpose. The kiln binds those particles together, so the end result is both strong and resilient. Each of us must endure the kiln.

We are His, not because of how well we endured trials, but to enable us to endure them.

Before surrendering their pottery to the kiln, the potters in Red Wing stamp their names in the clay. Did you know that God does that for us too? Second Corinthians 1:22 says that He "set his seal of ownership on us, and put his Spirit in our hearts." Amazingly, God set His seal of ownership on us *before* the kiln.

We are His, not because of how well we endured trials, but to enable us to endure them.

God equips each of us to fulfill the work He prepared for us to do (Ephesians 2:10). If God allows a hardship, it is so the kiln can weld qualities together to fulfill His plans in us. Our heavenly Potter has power over the kiln. He did not just monitor the furnace that held Shadrach, Meshach, and Abednego, but walked in the furnace with them (Daniel chapter 3).

Jesus is with us in the kiln—the pain and troubles of this world. We need not be afraid of the kiln God uses to strengthen us.

We can rejoice, too, when we run into problems and trials, for we know that they help us develop endurance. And endurance develops strength of character, and character strengthens our confident hope of salvation. And this hope will not lead to disappointment. For we know how dearly God loves us, because he has given us the Holy Spirit to fill our hearts with his love.

—Romans 5:3–5 (NLT)

When you feel the kiln's burn, may you also feel the Potter's hand and trust His heart.

Listen

Read 2 Corinthians 9:8
Declare it aloud if you can

At the furnace's door, Shadrach, Meshach, and Abednego declared God was able. When God permits you to endure the kiln, remember: He is with you. He is able. He is faithful. His purpose will prevail.

† Where is your kiln? Are you in it? Out of it? Or is it ahead of you?

† Is God protecting you from the kiln, preparing you for it, or is He in the kiln with you?

† As your day resumes, let God remind you of His faithfulness.

† Journal a prayer of gratitude for God's faithfulness through this day and night. Ask for His guiding hand for tomorrow.

LISTEN FOR HIS VOICE

An Apple a Day

For the word of God is alive and active.
Sharper than any double-edged sword,
it penetrates even to dividing soul and spirit, joints and marrow;
it judges the thoughts and attitudes of the heart.

—Hebrews 4:12

Apples are said to be the perfect fruit. They are packed with nutrients that help fight cancer, while facilitating weight loss and general health. However, the potential health benefits of an apple are totally useless unless that apple is inside you.

Likewise, to reap the benefits of God's Word, it must be implanted in your heart and mind. Psalm 1:2 talks about meditating on God's Word day and night. The word *meditate* used here means to chew on like a cow chewing cud. We cannot chew on something that is still sitting in the refrigerator.

> *We cannot chew on something that is still sitting in the refrigerator.*

To chew on God's Word, we must first put it in our minds and hearts. Psalm 119:11 says, "I have hidden your word in my heart that I might not sin against you." We cannot hide what has not been first acquired. When God's Word is alive and active in us, His Holy Spirit guides and protects our thoughts so that our words and actions bring God glory. We also gain greater insight into how deep God's love is for us. No apple a day can accomplish that.

The Bible was never designed to sit on the coffee table or occupy an hour of our Sunday or precede dessert at a weekly Bible study. That was never God's plan. God's Word is designed to be alive and active (Hebrews 4:12) until it returns to Him fulfilled, "So is my word that goes out from my mouth: It will not return to me empty, but will accomplish what I desire and achieve the purpose for which I sent it" (Isaiah 55:11).

Has Sunday's message ever evaporated like the morning dew before you left the church parking lot? Has its truth failed to penetrate deep enough to affect your thoughts, words, and actions throughout the week? What happens when a verse of Scripture fails its Isaiah mission? Does it return to God unfulfilled?

When Jesus taught his disciples how to pray, He included an interesting phrase: "Give us today our daily bread" (Matthew 6:11). God could have created our bodies so that consuming a sizable meal once a week would satisfy our needs. He did for many snakes, fish, crocodiles, lions, and other wild animals. However, He created our bodies to require daily increments of food.

While the process of ingesting our daily allotment of food requires a very small portion of our day, the food remains *active*. Throughout the day, our body absorbs vitamins and nutrients that enable it to grow, function, and sustain itself long after the meal is consumed. Similarly, God created our innermost being to require daily increments of His Word.

When Satan tempted Jesus in the wilderness, Jesus answered, "Man shall not live on bread alone, but on every word that comes from the mouth of God" (Matthew 4:4). Our body, mind, and soul require daily increments of God's Word to resist temptation and mature spiritually.

Whether we invest five minutes or several hours consuming God's Word, it remains alive and active. Thus, its Isaiah 55 mission to influence our responses to challenges, blessings, and other events that fill our days is fulfilled.

It would be insane for us to consume several gallons of milk on Sunday and expect sufficient calcium in our bones to sustain a fall. We would never consider consuming a large quantity of meat two times a year to fulfill our muscles' demand for protein. Likewise, even a fool would not take all seven multivitamins in one day and consider it a week's worth.

"Then Jesus declared, 'I am the bread of life. Whoever comes to me will never go hungry, and whoever believes in me will never be thirsty'" (John 6:35). Spiritually, we need God's Word daily to fortify our soul, so we can mature in our faith, resist sin, and be able to stand strong, even though we may periodically stumble along the way.

God's Word is always alive and active, but it is most alive and active in believers who faithfully plant His Word in their hearts, diligently listen for His voice, and courageously obey. While apples are loaded with nutrients our bodies need, God's Word is loaded with everything we need in this life and the next.

Listen

Read Matthew 6:11

Sometimes, focusing on each word provides a deeper insight to a familiar phrase: Give. Us. Today. Our. Daily. Bread.

✝ Give each word a synonym, reflection, or definition. (Like: Give: not earned; Today: not tomorrow; Our: meant to share; Daily: each day)

✝ How has God ministered to you in the past?

✝ What does He *give*? Why you? Why just one day? What is essential?

✝ As your day resumes, invite God to minister to you through these five words.

✝ Journal whatever God reveals to you this day and night while you savor a fresh bakery item, as if for the first time.

Truth Be Told

Instead, we will speak the truth in love,
growing in every way more and more like Christ,
who is the head of his body, the church.

—Ephesians 4:15 (NLT)

With painful familiarity, the scene unfolded between her and her husband. Another eruption. Another reminder that this was not the abundant life she heard preached so ardently on Sunday mornings. O, you of little faith, it taunted her, if you just had the faith of a mustard seed this would not be happening (Luke 17:6). But it was happening. Again.

She fought to control the gamut of emotions which demanded acknowledgement. It was exhausting. Empathy wrestled with self-preservation like rival advocates. Each justified their retaliation, while trampling any desire to confront the beast wreaking havoc on her marriage and life.

"Speak the truth in love" we are told in Ephesians 4:15. This is a triple command, not a suggestion: Speak. The truth. In love. Her self-preservation demanded the satisfaction that speaking the truth would provide. Alas, it was hopeless. Unless she fulfilled the triple command, God could not be glorified, nor His plan executed. Failure. Again.

Have you ever felt that way? You know the truth. Yet you also know any satisfaction in spitting it out would quickly evaporate and only intensify the stench of hurt and regret that already stings your eyes. Misunderstanding someone's understanding is normal in any relationship. Even when two become one, they are still two. Hurt hurts when we fail to see the other person.

But how can you promote understanding without inflicting more unintended pain? What can you do when everything you

> *But how can you promote understanding without inflicting more unintended pain?*

think, say, or do will be used against you in the court of their mindset? Speak. The truth. In love. How? Before we can speak the truth in love, we must define truth. We need to know the truth in love before we can speak in love.

TRUTH: It was a corporate ax-swing that no one anticipated. The ensuing emotional rollercoaster of interviews followed by rejections hacked at her husband's self-worth and confidence. It dwarfed the enemy in plain sight by drawing attention to symptoms rather than the real issue.

TRUTH: They were in this together. This did not just happen to him. Yet he turned a blind eye to how the loss of his job hurt her. If she wanted to go to bed in lieu of another episode on Netflix®, he hurled a slew of "Sure, rub it in! YOU have a job! All you think about is yourself! You belittle me every chance you get."

An inquiry about his day or an interview might spark, "Oh, stab the knife in and twist it. You love to humiliate me." But if she did not ask, then to him, she did not care and only thought of herself. Any casual comment was interpreted into something that was never intended, without any consideration for what she felt.

TRUTH: This was not what he wanted for them. Yet it never entered his mind how frustrating it was for her. It was a lonely kind of hard truth.

TRUTH: Compassion towards her husband and gratitude for her extra hours at work did not nullify the suffocating feeling of helplessness and frustration. Truth be told: The truth is that the truth was not enough.

IN LOVE: Everything within her yearned to speak the truth in love. He was not the only casualty in the downsizing ambush. She was too. For almost two decades, they sought to honor God with their commitment to each other and their marriage vows. The knowledge that God would bring them through this storm stronger was the ray of hope to which she clung. Thankfully, God's loving hand over her mouth prevented a catapult of destructive words, however truth-glazed they might be. Unspoken words scorched her throat as the truth wrestled to escape, but love permitted a silent surrender. Regardless of the frustrations hurled, she clung to the fact that she loved her husband and knew he loved her.

SPEAK: Was she expected to "speak the truth in love" knowing he was not able to receive it, neither in love nor as truth? Was she still obligated, knowing a remnant of truth would be twisted into destructive versions she never intended and thrown back at her?

The situation was demoralizing for him. He did not want pity, but her sympathy was not enough to comfort what needed confronting. She wanted to tell him how much it hurt her as well, but that would only come across as selfishness and supply him with more ammo for the next assault. She kept silent.

How could she justify verbalizing what she felt at the expense of inflicting more pain.

While she could empathize with how he felt, he felt no obligation to consider her feelings. How could she justify verbalizing what she felt at the expense of inflicting more pain onto an already grossly misplaced sense of failure? Did silence mean only his feelings mattered?

The struggle was real. Any justifiable solution felt wrong, yet fully justified at the same time. She turned to prayer. Prayer was all she could do, although it felt futile to pray when she was clueless what to pray for. If she vindicated herself, her words would hurt the person she loved. If she vindicated her husband, her silence devalued her feelings. Where was the justice?

"Lord, help me!" she prayed. "Whichever I choose feels wrong. I cannot speak and not speak at the same time. Help me, Lord. How can I obey Your command to speak truth in love?"

Engulfed in silence, her heart sensed the warmth of His hand upon her shoulder as a perplexing verse resounded in her heart's ear: "Do not throw your pearls before swine, lest they trample them under foot and turn to attack you" (Matthew 7:6 RSV).

Like a splash of ice water in the face, the oddity of the thought instantly demanded her full attention. Why had this verse emerged through the fog? Jesus warns His followers not to waste spiritual resources on people who would never appreciate them.

She could not see how it could apply to her situation. "Okay, Lord. You got my attention. What's up with the swine and pearls?"

> *The pearls were her feelings, which God deemed valuable beyond measure.*

Slowly, like a rose opening to release its fragrance, awareness crept into her heart. The pearls were her feelings, which God deemed valuable beyond measure. God heard her cry! She was not alone. God validated her feelings. He expected her to safeguard her pain until it was safe to share.

She let that truth seep into her soul. We are forbidden to allow anyone to carelessly trample our feelings underfoot or give someone the opportunity to use our words against us. God knew that at the time her feelings would be trampled upon. His command to "Speak the truth in love" had not changed. But she was commanded to safeguard her feelings, her "pearls," until her husband could hear the truth in love. What a blessed reminder to realize her feelings were precious to God. That she was precious to God!

We must never compromise speaking the truth in love. The triple command in Ephesians protects our relationships, and (when necessary) keeps God's hand over our mouths all to His glory. When we know our feelings are precious to God, He empowers us to be obedient, to pray for those who hurt us, and to wait for understanding when there seems to be no hope for it.

> *When we know our feelings are precious to God, He empowers us to be obedient.*

As she prayed for her husband and their marriage, God's assurance gave her confidence that maybe, in time, she could safely entrust her pearls to her husband in truth and in love. When that time came, or if it never did, God's vindication provided the love and courage she needed today. And that was enough.

Do you struggle with feeling undervalued? Does the risk of speaking the truth in love threaten to further alienate you from the one you desperately want to connect with? Remember, your pearls are valuable beyond measure to your heavenly Father. He has forbidden you to allow anyone to trample them underfoot or turn them against you. He will safeguard them with His arms around you.

Imagine, if you will, your pearls, your feelings and hurts and hopes, nestled in the loving hand of Our Father. Safe. Secure. Valued. Sometimes, He gently places the pearls into His jewelry box, never to be shared. Other times, He returns them to you when the time is right to speak the truth in love as part of the healing process, even though it might sting. I pray, dear friend, that the keeper of your pearls fills you with courage and wisdom to always speak truth in love.

Listen
Read Ephesians 4:15

This triple command serves a greater purpose than simply communicating our hurts. It is so that the one who speaks *and* the one who listens can grow more like Christ. If you missed that, read Ephesians 4:15 again. Breathe in His unfathomable love for you.

✝ When has someone spoken truth to you? Was it in love? Was it welcomed? What was the result? Does it still hurt?

✝ Is there is someone in your life who needs truth? Can you speak it in love? Will it be received in love? Is it truth? Are your pearls safe?

✝ As your day resumes, invite God to speak truth to you in His love. Be open for correction or conviction. Accept affirmation and comfort.

✝ Journal what God has spoken to you this day in His truth and in His Love.

Words and Deeds

Words and deeds, like little seeds,
Grow into flowers or to weeds.
We cannot help but when we pass,
To leave an imprint that will last.

Words can lift a fallen heart
Words can tear a world apart.
What will bloom in your footsteps?
What will outlast all the rest?

Will your words and deeds inspire?
Like flowers lifting spirits higher?
Or will weeds of dark oppression
Leave a wake of sure destruction?

Everyone contributes some.
It matters not if old or young.
To leave the world a better place
Cultivate some seeds of grace.

A neglected word or deed
Leaves room for weeds to succeed.
And choke words that could have been
Flowers of encouragement.

Like the tall, majestic pines,
Let your words be soft and kind.
Reaching high and reaching wide,
Let loving words in you abide.

E'er since life began in the garden
God planted seeds of love within
Each believer's heart and soul
To share His love where'er they go.

When God's love in you grows
Glorious blooms are sure to show.
So, let us all take special heed
To spread kind words and thoughts and deeds!

Listen

Read Ephesians 4:31–32

Throughout this day, your words and deeds will leave footprints. Some words need to be silenced. Sometimes a silence needs to be heard. A neglected word or deed can be destructive.

✝ How do your words and deeds reflect the person you want to be?

✝ Who needs encouragement? Who needs forgiveness?

✝ Encourage one person each day for one week. (seven days/seven people). Include yourself.

✝ Journal this day and night's words and deeds in your footsteps. Plan tomorrow's footprints.

LISTEN FOR HIS VOICE

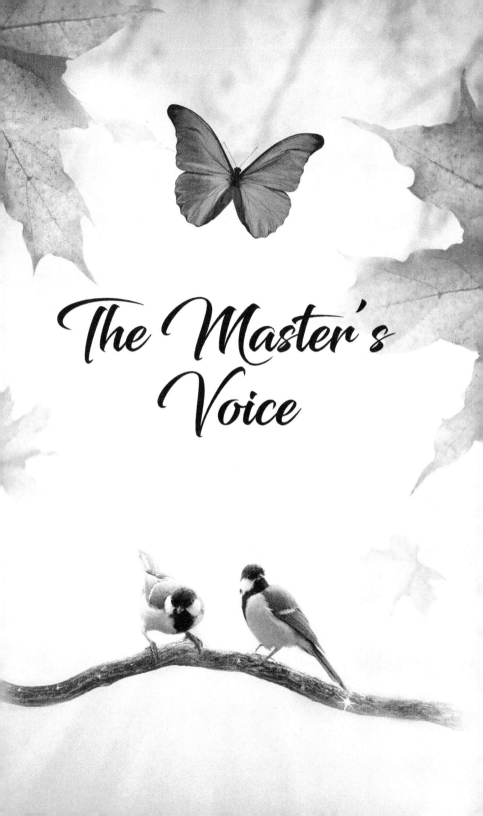

The Master's Voice

Miraculous Healings

His master replied, "Well done, good and faithful servant!
You have been faithful with a few things;
I will put you in charge of many things.
Come and share your master's happiness!"

—Matthew 25:21

An unresponsive laptop or cellphone can often be revived by disconnecting the power source, waiting a few minutes, then rebooting. The device's ability to self-repair is not contingent upon us understanding the code or technology involved. With a grateful sigh of relief, we acknowledge someone masterminded the instant fix and resume our day.

The human body is designed to repair itself too. Yet we rarely consider how masterfully God designed our bodies to heal without any direction from us. Certain organs and tissues can regenerate themselves. Of course, humans will never regrow an arm or tail like sea stars, salamanders, and geckos. Or regenerate a new claw like crabs. We can, however, regenerate bone and skin cells to repair or replace damage from cuts, burns, or breaks, regardless of each unique cell structure.

Did you know liver transplants require only half of the organ? It then regenerates itself in the recipient and donor, usually within a month. The speed and efficiency in which our body detects injury and activates aid without any direction from us is equally amazing.

A simple bump on the arm deploys our body's natural defense system to widen blood vessels and increase blood flow to the injured area. This extra blood warms the area causing white blood cells (leukocytes) to seep out of the capillaries to fight infection. All this action just under the skin causes the site to swell and creates the telltale black and blue bruise.

With minor cuts, healing occurs quickly without conscious effort or deliberate thought, so we fail to consider the miracle. No one posts on Facebook, "I got a paper cut this morning. Please pray for a miracle." We just squeeze some ointment onto a bandage, slap it on, and get on with our day. We fail to pray for the miracle because we fail to acknowledge our body was actively engaged in miraculous healing before we reached for the bandage.

Should we post prayer requests? Sure. Post them. Get the prayer warriors rolling. Then, let God get the glory even when the doctor says, "It appears the blood sample must have been contaminated. There is no sign of whatever in your blood." Or "Apparently the technician misread the X-rays because we can find no evidence the tumor ever existed." Praise be to doctors who call a miracle a miracle instead of attempting to explain God's intervening hand as an oversight.

> God can heal—every hurt, injury, and disease—yet when He chooses not to, we become discouraged and confused.

God can heal—every hurt, injury, and disease—yet when He chooses not to, we become discouraged and confused. When the miraculous healing we pray for does not happen, it is hard to see our bodies as living proof He designed us for everyday miracles. In many situations, it is hard to "Trust in the Lord with all your heart and lean not on your own understanding" (Proverbs 3:5).

How can you trust God to reveal a greater plan when the wrong words flow from the doctor's mouth? Maybe you want to trust in the Lord, but the future offers no solution, and you are staggering under the weight of today. Your desire to trust is strong, but the reality is you are suffocating with doubt and fear. You realize you are leaning on your own understanding. Yet without that, you would truly fall. Trust in the Lord, not your own understanding. Okay, you want to. But how do you "do" Proverbs 3:5?

> *Embrace the miracle that enables you to trust in the Lord instead of your own understanding.*

Here is a verse you might be familiar with: "His master replied, 'Well done, good and faithful servant! You have been faithful with a few things; I will put you in charge of many things. Come and share your master's happiness!'" (Matthew 25:21). Usually, we apply this verse to how we live. Have you ever thought of flipping it? Have you ever given a thought as to how God lives out this verse?

In the event of a cut on your finger, God faithfully designed your body to heal and regenerate itself without any assistance from you. If He is faithful in this small matter, can we fully trust Him with the bigger stuff? If He can create our world and the entire universe out of nothing, can we not fully trust Him to take care of us?

Yes! We can trust God with the small stuff we do not fully understand. Therefore, we can trust Him with the big stuff we have no hope of understanding. Proverbs 3:5 says trust in the Lord. Embrace the miracle that enables you to trust in the Lord instead of your own understanding. Rejoice in the miracles that happen within you without requiring any faith from you. And the next time you cut your finger, bruise your arm, or break a bone, remember that miraculous healing has been deployed even before you cry, "OUCH!"

Listen

Read Matthew 25:21

We are reminded to *remember* over 250 times throughout the Scriptures because we tend to forget. Sometimes, God works quietly behind the scenes. Other times, He works boldly, even miraculously.

† What has God done for you? Big or small? Recently or in the distant past?

† Has He worked in response to prayer or without your asking?

† As your day resumes, be aware of God's presence— past or present.

† Journal whatever God reveals throughout this day and night.

See **Listen for More**, page 234 for additional information about miraculous healings that happen every day.

Spiritual Whiskers

For the eyes of the Lord range throughout the earth
to strengthen those whose hearts are fully committed to him.

—2 Chronicles 16:9

It was an intriguing title: *How to Clicker Train Your Cat.* The combination of cat and train without the word *impossible* sparked my curiosity. What would our feline queen, Denali, think of clicker training? Armed with a clicker in one hand, treats in the other, I held out the eraser end of a pencil and waited . . . and waited . . . and waited.

Despite attempts to ignore the intrusion, curiosity eventually propelled her nose forward for a sniff. Click. Treat. Just like the book said. Perplexed, Denali enjoyed the unexpected morsel as she wondered what happened. When the pencil presented itself again, her nose touched it. Click. Another treat. Wow. We were equally amazed.

Within days, she unreservedly jumped from one platform to another. It was not long before the pencil was replaced with a finger point and butt rubs became her preferred reward. Although in violation of the feline code of ethics, Denali thoroughly loved our new game. But only as long as it suited her mood. Therein laid the secret.

Interpreting the cat's interest is critical to successful clicker training. It enables you to engage when there is interest and to quit before it fades. This is much easier than it sounds since cats encompass their entire being into whatever captures their attention. Which is why they are so comical when startled during a stalk.

To avoid detection, many hunting animals minimize movement, while maximizing surveillance with a cocked ear, inquisitive sniff of the air, and the feel of surrounding vibrations through their feet. In low light, pupils widen so more light is collected, revealing additional information. Cats, however, possess unique visual abilities independent of available light. Their vertical pupils widen whenever interest demands and narrow as interest diminishes.

If you have a cat, try this experiment. When your cat is lying quietly, position yourself in front of its face. Wait for it to return to the relaxed "whatever" stage, then present an object like a feather. If interested, the pupils widen even though the lighting has not changed. After a while, when the object does nothing, interest fades and the pupils narrow. If a twitch reignites interest, the pupils widen again, independent of lighting conditions.

However, you do not have to get in their face to figure out if they are interested or not. Felines' unique whiskers unveil additional information to assist the careful observer as to the direction of whatever has captured their interest.

Ultra-sensitive whiskers extend the width of their shoulders to instantly appraise when a passageway is too narrow. That is why only fat cats get stuck in unlikely places. But those whiskers also disclose the slightest shift of interest regardless of whether it is a mouse, feather, finger point, or even itself, a cat's whiskers point towards their current interest.

As long as the object is interesting, the whiskers point toward it. When it becomes boring, the whiskers drift backwards, towards default: self. For the feline, interest in anything other than self is always temporary. Repeat the same experiment but this time, observe the whiskers. They reveal direction of interest and intensity.

Because we did not speak the same language, the clicker-reward method helped Denali discern what I expected from her. However, her whiskers helped me discern the direction of her attention. They also enabled me to detect the slightest shift in interest, so I ended the game before she made that call.

Does the language barrier between you and God ever feel as foreign as it did between Denali and me? Isaiah 55:9 contains this lament: "As the heavens are higher than the earth, so are my ways higher than your ways and my thoughts than your thoughts."

Does God speak a different language so that some spiritual clicker-reward system is required for us to understand Him? And along that note, would there be any type of "spiritual whiskers" that might reveal, like Denali's did, whether we were even aware of God's "finger point" or "clicker"?

Suddenly a simple game with my cat became a spiritual awareness assessment for which I feared I might fail. Yet at the same time, I realized that failure to be aware of failing would have far greater consequences. With quivering steps, assessing my *spiritual whiskers* became essential. If I examined my own heart, what would the direction of my "whiskers" reveal about my interest in God's plan?

> *Failure to be aware of failing would have far greater consequences.*

My first question was, does God speak a different language so we have no hope of understanding Him? If we are created in His image and likeness as it says in Genesis 1:26, then unlike my feline friend, the language barrier is nonexistent. Through His Word, God simply and clearly communicates what He expects of us:

✝ "He has shown you, O mortal, what is good. And what does the Lord require of you? To act justly and to love mercy and to walk humbly with your God" (Micah 6:8).

✝ "Observe what the Lord your God requires: Walk in obedience to him and keep his decrees and commands, his laws and regulations as written in the Law of Moses. Do this so you may prosper in all you do and wherever you go" (1 Kings 2:3).

✝ "Love your enemies, do good to them" (Luke 6:35).

We all have limited discernment. Have you ever prayed for the gift of discernment so that you can understand God's plan? King David did in Psalm 119:125. "I am your servant, give me discernment that I may understand your statutes." God gives us discernment to understand His ways while He observes our "spiritual whiskers." When our "whiskers" reveal our heart's desire to obey, God fortifies that desire so we can be more fully committed to Him. "For the eyes of the Lord range throughout the earth to strengthen those whose hearts are fully committed to him" (2 Chronicles 16:9).

> God gives us discernment to understand His ways while He observes our "spiritual whiskers."

Without the desire to obey, discernment is useless. Denali quickly learned to discern what was expected. Surprisingly, she felt so compelled to touch my finger point that when the game did not suit her mood, she physically turned her head away from me—sometimes her entire body. I guess in the feline mind, it is not disobedience if you do not actually *see* the command. Whatever.

When fully engaged in our game, Denali directed her focus, eyes, and whiskers towards me. However, once her whiskers drifted towards herself, obedience in her mind became optional. "Seriously," she seemed to say, "I cannot see how that command applies to me." Which made me wonder: when God observed my heart's "spiritual whiskers," what did they reveal?

Did my "whiskers" point toward where God was leading or toward doing things my way? Daily investment in God's Word helped me to stay tuned to what God desired and more compelled to obey His promptings. However, when life got busy, scheduling time in His Word felt optional. The compelling force to do the right thing for the right reason at the right time began to fade as my desire to obey dwindled until I failed to see how it applied to me.

Sometimes Denali's overpowering natural desire to live by her terms compelled her to turn away from me. She chose to ignore my command regardless of any potential reward. Did my sinful nature compel me to do the same thing to the Lord, my God?

Without the desire to obey, discernment is useless.

The Old Testament contains a comical visual (at least it would be comical if it were not true) of what this looks like: "Your ancestors refused to listen to this message. They stubbornly turned away and put their fingers in their ears to keep from hearing... That is why the Lord of Heaven's Armies was so angry with them" (Zechariah 7:11–18 NLT).

When do we stick our fingers in our ears? When we fail to see the clerk who needs a cheerful word. Whenever we justify careless words regardless of the pain they inflict. When we refuse to value whatever good could have been accomplished, choosing instead our sinful default nature—self. Instead, we forfeit the multidimensional rewards God intends, as our selfishness celebrates its own shortsighted compensation and the Lord, our God, is disappointed with us.

No one expects a feline to willingly obey a finger point. It is, after all, pointless. When Denali turned her face from me, the only negative impact was a forfeited butt rub. But God expects obedience. In fact, He expects even our thoughts to be obedient

> *When we turn our backs
> to God's promptings, we
> miss the opportunity
> to be a vessel through
> which God intended to
> bless someone else.*

to Him. "Take captive every thought to make it obedient to Christ" (2 Corinthians 10:5).

When we turn our backs to God's promptings, we miss the opportunity to be a vessel through which God intended to bless someone else. We prevent His blessing from pouring forth upon our world. Unfortunately, we also forfeit the peace of mind, joy, fulfillment, and fellowship the Lord wants to bestow upon us. Ultimately, we risk forfeiting one of the most amazing rewards available to believers:

> But whenever anyone turns to the Lord, the veil is taken away. Now the Lord is the Spirit, and where the Spirit of the Lord is, there is freedom. And we all, who with unveiled faces contemplate the Lord's glory, are being transformed into his image with ever-increasing glory, which comes from the Lord, who is the Spirit.—2 Corinthians 3:16–18

Imagine how it must grieve the heart of God when His grace and blessings are wasted. When we turn our face away, we forfeit experiencing His transforming power with its "ever-increasing glory."

There were times when Denali struggled with feline me-first syndrome and her head turned away. Yet, one ear and a few whiskers remain focused on me. A twitch might entice her back into the game. Or not. Eventually desire determined her reward: butt rub or self-satisfaction. Whenever our sinful nature causes us to drift, God initiates a twitch to recapture our attention. He might use a song on the radio or a quiet whisper in our heart so our "spiritual whiskers" can rotate back towards Him before our sinful self-default forfeits His reward.

Sometimes, a verse of Scripture or the words of a friend will encourage, comfort, or lovingly rebuke us. Being aware of our "spiritual whiskers" helps us stay focused on God's "finger point." Our ultimate reward far exceeds any self-administered prize. I truly believe Paul's words in 1 Corinthians 2:9 that "No eye has seen, no ear has heard, and no mind has imagined what God has prepared for those who love him" (NLT). We cannot even imagine the grand rewards God has prepared for those whose "spiritual whiskers" are focused on the Lord and His mighty power. Be prepared to be amazed.

Lord, when I am like Miss Denali and turn my heart away from you, please get in my face so I am compelled to obey. Fill me with the desire to obey. Help me see the clerk that needs a cheerful word. Replace my careless words with encouragement. Help me desire the goodness only obedience can accomplish. Teach me to capture my thoughts and make them obedient to You so my greatest reward will be in You. Let me rest in You. Abide in You. Inspire me to obey Your command so that I can glorify You with honor and praise all my days. Lavish me with Your extravagant love beyond my wildest imagination. Amen. (Inspired by 2 Corinthians 10:5; 1 John 3:1).

Listen

Read 2 Corinthians 10:5 and Philippians 4:8

How do you capture your thoughts and make them obedient to Christ? Put them through the Philippians 4:8 filter. Is it true, noble, right, pure, lovely, admirable, excellent, or praiseworthy? Invite God to assist you.

† How is your obedience meter? What do your "spiritual whiskers" reveal?

† What rules should be suggestions? (Speed limits? Ten commandments? No strollers on escalators? Don't sit on a cactus? Read your Bible daily?)

† When you take your thoughts captive, what does Philippians 4:8 obedience look like?

† Journal your "whisker" assessment and adjustments that God addressed this day and night. Make tangible plans for tomorrow's obedience.

LISTEN FOR HIS VOICE

To Know Her is to Love Her

The King will reply, "Truly I tell you,
whatever you did for one of the least of these
brothers and sisters of mine, you did for me."

—Matthew 25:40

"S he was a talented seamstress, avid fisherman, master gardener, dedicated nurse. I remember when ..." The eulogies spoken paid tribute to sixty years of fond memories while avoiding eye contact with the elephant in the room.

My mother was all these things. Every word was true. But she was also a drunk and drug addict who deprived her children of a stable home. She allowed her addiction to destroy relationships as surely as it destroyed her body. Will whatever good she accomplished on this earth be forever tarnished by the pain she inflicted upon those God entrusted into her care?

Have you ever been wounded so deeply it is a struggle to acknowledge the good? Does forgiveness gurgle within until it surfaces like a belch to sting your soul and leave a bitter taste in your mouth? You are not alone. It matters not if your struggle condemns the perpetrator or if it condemns you for feeling that way. It is a trap with no positive escape.

"To know her is to love her."[1] Applying those seven iconic words to my mother haunted me for years. If only I could un-hear them. As her daughter, I followed God's command to "honor your father and mother." I treated her with kindness and respect. But to love her was unbearable—and impossible (or so I thought).

> How can we claim to truly love someone if we choose to cherish only the good and refuse to accept their flaws?

How can we claim to truly love someone if we choose to cherish only the good and refuse to accept their flaws? Can we ever hope to really love someone without knowing them and not love them selectively, but completely?

So, what does "To know her is to love her" really mean? God knew my mother intimately and completely. And He loved her. He loved her enough to send His only Son. He loved her enough to nail her sin to the cross of salvation.

Jesus did not lay down His life because of whatever good we have done nor simply to pay for our sin. Jesus loves us just as we are—the good, the bad and the hidden. Romans 5:8 says, "But God demonstrates his own love for us in this: While we were still sinners, Christ died for us."

Ultimately, Love loves. God can love the sinner without compromising His disdain for sin. That is comforting unless the expectation also applies to us. Especially when applied towards those who have hurt us deeply.

God loved my mom. But He is God. We can expect impossible things from God. The Bible challenged us with, "Whoever does not love does not know God, because God is love" (1 John 4:8). Does God really expect us to love like He does?

It was a random Sunday message designed to encourage the congregation to actively serve their community with a food and clothing drive. "The King will reply, 'Truly I tell you, whatever you did for one of the least of these brothers and sisters of mine, you did for me'" (Matthew 25:40). The preacher's words landed like a thud in my heart. I could hardly breathe and my knees threatened to crumble under me.

Has a tune ever danced in your head regardless of how much you tried to shake it? Has a verse ever danced in your heart with conviction regardless of your arguments that it does not apply to you? That is what this verse did to me.

The Lord got personal. A whisper in my heart challenged me to love my *least*. There was no denying the conviction that my *least* was my mother. I argued that the verse applied to those who were powerless, those with no food, water, clothing, or were in prison. But my arguments ricocheted back at me. "It is easy to love someone who has never hurt you. It feels good to give without recognition to a stranger. Are they the least for you?" the Lord asked my heart, "Who is on your 'anyone except' list?"

God cares how we love the one we love the least.

God cares how we love the one we love *the least*. God cares about that person on our "anyone except" list as much as He cares for you and me and those without food, water, clothing, or who are in prison. But how do you separate decades of abuse, hurt, and disappointment to love someone like Jesus did? You can't. But God can. We only love God because He first loved us (1 John 4:19). It is His love, His divine intervention, that can enable us to love someone whom He loved first.

For many years I have thought of that day: standing by my mom's coffin and remembering her life. I prayed for a deep penetrating hurt, an aching void that refused to be denied. As odd as it might seem, I desperately wanted the pain, the void, the ache in my heart at her passing that only love can bring. I prayed to be gripped with soul-wrenching grief rather than breathing a gentle sigh of relief.

That might sound like a strange prayer. After all, I knew many of her darkest secrets and her impressive accomplishments. I understood most of her greatest joys and deepest fears. Together we faced failures and celebrated successes.

But I had also lived with the pain, frustration, and hopelessness of her substance abuse. My greatest fear had been that her death would bring relief instead of grief. I greatly desired the stinging pain of loss over any grateful sense of liberation.

Without realizing it, I had asked God to allow me to know my mom and to love her so His love could create the aching void I now feel. To know my mom and love her, I needed to forgive her. That was not possible for me to do. So, God revealed a tiny secret He tucked into the word forgive. *Give*. What I felt unable to forgive, I had to give to God. That freed me to love my mother as He loved her.

God taught me how to love my mother. To love all of her. Not selectively. Not overlooking her faults. Not just forgiving offenses against me and my siblings. Not just loving the good stuff. But to truly love her as she was. Not who I thought she should have been.

I will be forever grateful God heard my cry. Today, I can honestly say I grieve the loss of my friend far more than lament the mother I never had.

There is a void in each of our hearts that only Jesus can fill. Only Jesus can heal the scars that might prevent God's love and forgiveness from entering. Only God can open our hearts to forgive the unforgivable and love the unlovable. Only with God can we love the one we consider the least.

"To know her is to love her." Gratefully, God answered my

> *May your heart be filled with gratitude when loss consumes your soul, realizing you are fully known and fully loved.*

prayer. I miss my mother. I am grateful to have known her and loved her. All of her. But even more, I am eternally grateful God knows you and me completely. Unreservedly. Unashamedly. I am "the least of these," yet He loves me enough to prepare a place for me in heaven and pay the price of admission. And not just for me—for anyone who calls on His Name. May your heart be filled with gratitude when loss consumes your soul, realizing you are fully known and fully loved.

Then the King will say to those on his right, "Come, you who are blessed by my Father; take your inheritance, the kingdom prepared for you since the creation of the world."

—Matthew 25:34

Listen

Read Matthew 25:40

After God revealed my *least*, it took a long while to honestly love my mother as God expected me to. Love for God is always first. We cannot love our least without God's love in us. If you feel convicted, that is a good thing. Loving your least takes time. Let God fill you with His love so you can overcome. Forgiveness does not right the wrong; it defuses its power. Intentional forgiveness often requires multiple applications. Be patient with yourself.

✝ Who are your "least of these"? Who is on your I-will-do-anything-for-anyone-*except* list? This could be a group of people or someone specific.

✝ As your day resumes, ask God to reveal the "least of these" you encounter like that person who drifted into your lane, put ketchup on your no-ketchup burger, slurped their soup, or was inconsiderate.

✝ Pray specifically: God, please help me to love _____.

✝ Journal the "least of these" that have been revealed this day and night.

Need divine assistance to overcome a *least*? The prayer below is a good start.

For God so loved _____ that He gave His only Son so that if he/she believes in Him, they will not perish, but have everlasting life. Jesus did not come into the world to condemn _____ but that _____, through Him, might be saved. Remind me that I and my least are fully known and fully loved by You. Fill me with Your love. In Jesus' name. Amen (Based on John 3:16–17).

Abiding Leash

I am the vine, you are the branches.
He who abides in Me, and I in him, bears much fruit;
for without Me you can do nothing.

—John 15:5 (NKJV)

After months of compromising on everything from carpet to the toothbrush drawer, we agreed our first home needed a dog to be complete. We decided to begin our search at the Animal Humane Society. During the 1970s, only a few rescue organizations existed. Because of our conflicting work schedules, I attended the Humane Society's Open House alone.

Dozens of tails wagged, but none matched our profile. Disappointed, I decided to leave when a forlorn creature caught my eye. Out of sympathy, I gently spoke to her, "You poor pathetic thing. Who would ever adopt you? Can you at least try to look a little optimistic?" Cautiously, she approached and licked my hand.

"Oh, you don't want that one," the attendant advised. "She is hopeless. The dog we rescued with her was put down last week. They were both severely abused. He was so aggressive, he literally bit the hand that fed him. Twice. No real hope for this one either."

She met only two qualifications on our profile: a rescue and mixed breed. "Can I bring my husband tomorrow to meet her?" I asked, not sure if he would bother to come with me. She did not even have a tail.

"I am sorry. She is scheduled to be euthanized tomorrow morning. I told you, she is hopeless." Her soft brown eyes pleaded for a chance to prove him wrong.

We changed her name to Lady and gave our Aussie mix a chance. Many rescued dogs enthusiastically embrace their new life, shredding their past like a snake sheds its skin. Lady was not one of them. Every movement, every object, seemed to sabotage any progress towards a redeemed life. Her old life haunted her.

Why did living righteously feel like a futile attempt to please an ever-demanding God?

Gradually, she learned to trust us to throw a ball or stick. The leash, however, possessed a power no game could overcome. It was like deep emotional wounds were ripped open just as they started to heal. Frustrated I prayed, "Lord, help me. How can I teach her the leash is her ally? Help me convince her it is useful to teach, correct, and train."

I wondered why those words sounded familiar. Then it occurred to me that Paul used them to describe God's Word, the Bible: "All Scripture is God-breathed and is useful for teaching, rebuking, correcting and training in righteousness" (2 Timothy 3:16). While it seemed sacrilegious to compare the Bible to a dog leash, the thought persisted like a song you cannot shake. Could there be a correlation between a leather dog leash and a leather-covered Bible?

How a dog reacts to the leash is often a good indicator of its relationship with its master. Some dogs love the leash. "Yippy, skippy, time for a walk or go bye-bye." Other dogs tug on the leash like a helium balloon poised for takeoff. Couch-potato pooches look at the leash and think, "Aww, do we have to?" Lady despised the leash because her cruel master used it to rebuke, instead of to teach. He used it to force her close but failed to draw her near.

Have you ever wanted the truth regardless of what it exposed? Have you wrestled with questions that ripped your heart open? As I reflected on my role as Lady's master, I had to ask myself,

Is God my Master or not? What did my response to His Word reveal about my relationship with Him? Why did cramming thirty minutes of Bible study into my day feel like one more dreaded chore on an endless to-do list? Why did I balk when a passage convicted me of some minor offense that God in His mercy could easily overlook? Did I really believe that is what grace is for? Why did living righteously feel like a futile attempt to please an ever-demanding God? I was ashamed. This was not the relationship I desired.

Lady's response to her first master was understandable. But I cannot justify these same feelings toward mine. Was God as dismayed at my reaction to His Word as I was to Lady's reaction to the leash in my hand?

Before I could transform Lady's association with the leash, I needed to deepen my relationship with her. Likewise, if I wanted to transform my association with God's Word, I had to focus on my relationship with Him.

While I gladly provided food, medical care, training, and exercise, I did not want Lady to view me solely as her meal ticket or source of fun.

> *If I wanted to transform my association with God's Word, I had to focus on my relationship with Him.*

The leash could teach her how to heel, but only time together would deepen our relationship to ignite a *desire* to heel.

Was God just my meal ticket? Just my provider? Just someone to answer my prayers? No wonder the Bible made me cringe. My relationship with my Master was shallow and distant. I knew what was expected but had no desire to obey. Unlike Lady, I had no justifiable reason for my attitude.

Lady learned to heel on our long walks together as our relationship deepened. Soon, her desire to trust me made obedience as natural as chasing squirrels. In the dog's world, it is called heel. In the Bible it is called *abide*.

Jesus used the word *abide* with the vine and the branches to define our relationship with God (John 15:5). *Abide* acknowledges the flow is from Jesus (the vine) to me (the branch) so the fruit is never about what I do, but what the vine enables me to produce. A branch receives life and the ability to produce fruit from the vine, not independent of it.

God designed many plants, including grapevines, to propagate via rooting a branch. Jesus, however, used the Greek word for join or abide which refers to grafting a branch to a vine or tree. The branch must accept its new life—and abide with the vine—or it will perish.

> Abide *emphasizes the vine's ability to give life, rather than the branch's willingness to receive it.*

Abide emphasizes the vine's ability to give life, rather than the branch's willingness to receive it. Jesus says, "I am the vine, you are the branches. He who abides in Me, and I in him, bears much fruit; for without Me you can do nothing" (John 15:5 NKJV). Unless we abide in the vine, our fruit yields nothing of eternal value.

For Lady, the leash was the graft; it connected the two of us. Grafts require time before they become a part of the vine. Lady and I took many walks together. We trained, played games, and watched ducks on the lake.

Eventually, the painful association with the leash was transformed. Instead of quivering in fear at the sight of it, she quivered with excitement. Her ears became so tuned to the sound of her leash that she would come running if my husband or I accidentally bumped it.

Lady triumphed when the dreaded leash was transformed into an abiding leash. The transformation of my attitude toward my Lord took time. Time in His Word. Time in prayer. Time just being still. Time watching ducks on the lake. Eventually, I eagerly sought time with my Lord, hungry for His wisdom, grateful for His rebuke, eagerly abiding in His love so my thoughts, words, and actions were in step with the Bible—His abiding leash.

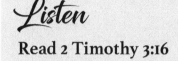

Read 2 Timothy 3:16

Take an honest evaluation of your response and attitude toward time in God's Word, church, or prayer.

- † How accurately does your response and attitude toward God's Word, church, or prayer reflect your relationship with God, your attitude toward His rebuke, or the relationship you desire?

- † As your day resumes, listen for God's comfort, rebuke, guidance, and love. Ask Him to remind you of His presence today and in the past.

- † Write a prayer of your desire or commitment to invest time in His Word.

- † Journal how God used this day and night to strengthen your relationship with Him.

LISTEN FOR HIS VOICE

The Green Football

With his green football and a waggin' tail
He greets me at the door without fail.
It has been a long day waiting patiently
For my presence to make his world complete.

There is no judgment in his heart or face.
Why can't we model this kind of grace?
Each day he greets me with such devotion.
It soothes my soul like an expensive lotion.

His green football I hold in my hand
Transforms my spirit like a magician.
Flee from me, all you troubles of today.
A pair of brown eyes begs me to play!

Whether we have parted for minutes or hours.
Whether I am rich or have not a dollar.
I am his master; he yearns for my touch.
Do I love my Lord and Master this much?

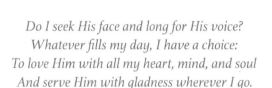

Do I seek His face and long for His voice?
Whatever fills my day, I have a choice:
To love Him with all my heart, mind, and soul
And serve Him with gladness wherever I go.

What hinders my desire to obey?
He provides for me each and every day.
Not just my needs, but my deepest desires.
Freely He gives what cannot be acquired.

What have I learned from my four-legged friend?
My Lord loves me so I can love Him.
I give Him my day like a green football.
Rejoice in His presence—and answer His call.

For He is My Lord, Master, and King
Who desires my love more than anything!
Help me to love You with heart, mind, and soul.
Secure in Your love wherever I go!

Inspiration for "The Green Football," is Revelation 4:10,
"They lay their crowns before the throne."

Chopper, our German Shepherd rescue dog inspired this poem. Details of his former abusive life are sketchy. He was determined to leave it behind to embrace the fresh start we offered. We have no idea why he picked up this custom, but early in his tenure he began greeting us with his green football. It was always near, never played with or chewed on. We could depend on his greeting in the morning when we awoke, upon returning home, or coming up the stairs after switching a load of laundry. He even fetched it upon hearing my voice on the phone.

Why Chops chose a green football, we will never know. And we will never know why it was not allowed to have the squeaker. After he ripped it from his first one, I threw that football away. His frantic but futile search engulfed him for days. Finally, I relented and replaced it. With a delighted sigh of relief, he promptly removed the second squeaker. Was the squeaker a distraction? Was it a temptation to play? I will never know for sure.

What "green footballs" has God given to you so that you can greet Him with a grateful heart? Have you thanked Him for the sunset? Do your eyes search for His handiwork so that you can give Him praise? Do you use the breath He has given you to worship His name? With his green football, Chops taught me to stay alert for opportunities to greet my Lord. To get rid of distractions so I can pause a moment to give God my full attention. To see His smile in the flower, hear His laughter in a squirrel's antics, or feel the warmth of His love on my face.

Life's highs, lows, and mundane of every day can interfere with our gratitude and attitude towards the One who has given us more than we could ever ask for. We love God only because He first loved us (1 John 4:19). The green football Chops greeted me with, I gave to him. Likewise, we will someday lay down a crown of glory that we received from God (1 Peter 5:4).

Chops faithfully took advantage of every opportunity to greet me with his green football. What if we were faithful to take advantage of every opportunity to greet our Lord with a grateful heart? What if that became so natural it required no forethought? What if we greeted each sunrise with, "Good morning, Lord"? Think of God's smile if our frequent greeting is "Hello, Lord, good to see You today."

Chops' greeting reminds us that one day we will greet our Lord and Master. Revelation provides a vision where we lay down our crowns before God's throne (Revelation 4:10). That scene might be intimidating—unless, like Chops, it was our normal routine. Imagine approaching God's throne in heaven and seeing a mile-high pile of "green footballs."

Listen

Read 1 Peter 5:4

Listen to Chris Tomlin sing "We Fall Down" on YouTube[1]. One day you will stand before God's throne in heaven and cry, "Holy, Holy, Holy." The word *holy* means "set apart." Until then, imagine if you set apart a holy breath to greet your Lord like Chops' green football. "Wow, Lord, that is a glorious sunrise." Imagine how much God would enjoy these holy greetings throughout His day.

✝ What distractions must be removed like Chops' squeaker?

✝ As your day resumes, take advantage of every opportunity to express a holy gratitude, love, and praise to God. How are you *set apart* from the world?

✝ Imagine what you might say when you lay down your crown before God's throne.

✝ Journal what God reveals to you this holy (*set apart*) day and night.

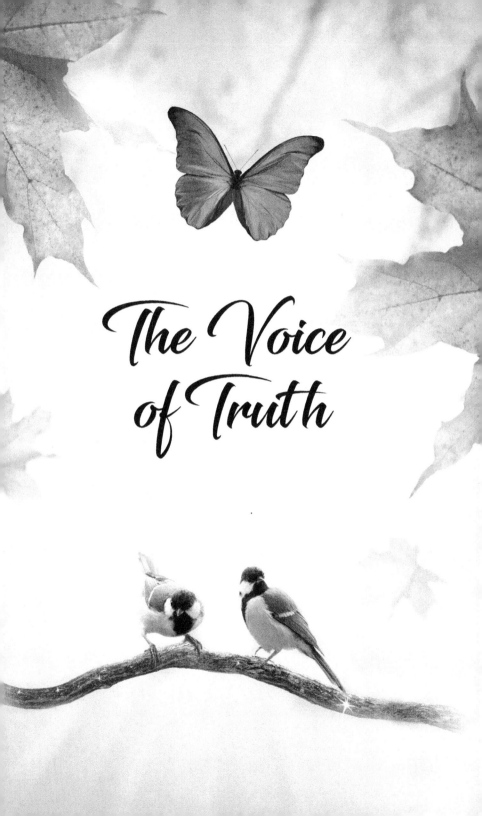

The Voice of Truth

Smitten by Mittens

For you created my inmost being;
you knit me together in my mother's womb.
I praise you because I am fearfully and wonderfully made;
your works are wonderful, I know that full well.

—Psalm 139:13–14

A n unnerving shudder escaped his broad shoulders. The young veterinary intern managed to keep his voice calm, yet his prognosis only further distorted the unfathomable scene.

"She has a gross deformity known as *polydactyl*." He spat the word out as if the thought of it residing on his tongue was nauseating. His repulsive grimace, suggesting that our adorable kitten was some kind of copy-paste malfunction, was scandalous. "Her right paw is the worst I have seen, but luckily she is young. In fact, at this age, these offensive extrusions can be surgically removed with virtually no visible scarring. Then she will be perfectly normal. How soon would you like to schedule that?"

I was appalled! Gross deformity? *Then* she would be perfectly normal? The words resounded off a defensive wall of disbelief. How dare he refer to those adorable, oversized paws with such disdain. Struggling to maintain composure, he politely awaited my answer. His gaze purposely diverted to avoid the gross deformities he was so anxious to amputate.

Have you ever thought something was endearing that someone else considered offensive? Iguanas. Snakes. Cats. Sushi. Cilantro.

Peppers. Mushrooms. Anchovies. Bell-bottom jeans. Tattoos. Does opinion determine value? Expecting the young veterinarian to comprehend how precious those abnormal paws were to us was as futile as expecting me to consider them repulsive.

Just a few weeks earlier, even in the dim lit barn cuddled in her mother's warmth, it was impossible to miss those massive paws attached to her petite body. The young vet called them *polydactyl*. *Poly* meaning "many" plus *dactyl* meaning "digits." According to legends, sailors in the 1600s believed these "deformed" cats brought luck on the high seas. More likely, their extra toes provided supreme agility on the riggings and made them top-notch rodent hunters.

Polydactyl cats have captured many hearts. Ernest Hemingway was extremely fond of them.[1] President Theodore Roosevelt's polydactyl cat, Slippers, roamed the White House.[2] And then, of course, us! We named her Little Denali, meaning little great one. With intense blue eyes, our tricolored cali-tabby would be a feline who prevailed beyond the cute stage. Yes! We were smitten by her mittens. The same mittens this fresh-from-med-school-intern found so repulsive.

> *His educated and medically influenced analysis was profoundly wrong on so many levels, as far as I was concerned.*

The vet was right. She was not normal. With a comical walk, she maneuvered those king-sized paws with her elfin body. If amputating one of her most endearing features would make her normal, then normal was not our desire.

As far as I was concerned, his educated and medically influenced analysis was profoundly wrong on so many levels. I snatched her tiny body from the clutch of his condemning fingers to reassure her that the deformity he so callously addressed was precious beyond words. As if she could comprehend, I whispered in her ear, "Do not worry, Denali, what he sees as repulsive, makes you uniquely special. Worry not, little great one, you do not need to be fixed. You are already perfect."

Calmed by Denali's rhythmic purring, I glanced up and froze. Standing in front of me—as real as it was surreal—was Jesus, with a rumpled-haired child snuggled onto His shoulder. I held Denali while the vet watched. And Jesus held the child while I watched. It was as real as if it had been real.

Jesus gazed at me and nodded. He affirmed my protective grip on Denali. I felt vindicated. The vet was wrong.

The parallel scenes resumed, strangely familiar yet totally foreign at the same time. I held Denali under the young veterinarian's repulsive glare. In the mirrored image, the child in Jesus' arms looked up at me with a confident smile on a severely deformed face. In horror, I watched myself recoil, replicating the young vet's reaction to Little Denali. "I would never!" my heart screamed. But I had. I diverted my gaze away from the child just like the vet had diverted his gaze away from Denali. Ashamed and appalled at my reaction, my heart wept, "O my Lord, forgive me."

"As the heavens are higher than the earth, so are my ways higher than your ways and my thoughts than your thoughts," says the Lord in Isaiah 55:9. Sometimes God's thoughts are so lofty that the human mind has no hope to comprehend the depth of His love. In that instant, I was acutely aware that as appalled as I was at the intern's reaction to Denali, it was microscopic compared to how appalled God must be when we treat His precious children with similar disdain.

King David expressed it well. "For you created my inmost being; you knit me together in my mother's womb. I praise you because I am fearfully and wonderfully made; your works are wonderful, I know that full well" (Psalm 139:13–14).

Although mortified to witness my reaction to someone else's imperfection, I am grateful it opened my eyes to a more godly perspective on perfection. I realized the words King David wrote include me and my imperfections, my so-called deformities. I cannot say I know it full well, but I understand it better.

Gently, Jesus comforted me in that parallel scene, "Now can you see how I love them? They are perfect. Not 'special needs' but special. They are not perfect despite their disability but because

> What people find hard to accept is the very thing that makes them uniquely special to Me.

of it. In fact, what people find hard to accept is the very thing that makes them uniquely special to Me. Oh, how I love them! Do you understand?"

Whether you find them endearing or repulsive, there is no denying Denali's jumbo paws. Likewise, you cannot help but notice someone who is affected with a deformity. The problem is, sometimes that is all we see, instead of a person fearfully and wonderfully made.

Denali never grew into those paws, which thundered across the floor to administer a mighty slap in pursuit of toys. No amount of medical knowledge will alter the fact that we were smitten by her mittens. Given enough time, that zealous young veterinary intern might likewise find them endearing. Thankfully, God does not need time to learn to love us. He is the same yesterday, today, and tomorrow. He cannot love us more, and He cannot love us less. His love is unconditionally unconditional.

While upon this earth, we will never fully understand the depth of God's love. But this encounter helped me appreciate imperfections as God's design regardless of what society is comfortable with.

We envision heaven as a perfect world, with perfect bodies, glorifying God. When you entertain thoughts of your glorified body, is it young, skinny, pretty, handsome, muscular, athletic, or with extra toes? Why do we think God has to fix our imperfections before we can enjoy eternity with him in heaven? God used a simple visit to the vet to reveal His heart so that it could change mine.

Then, as if the whole experience required a "last reveal" to affirm this revelation, one more surprise awaited me at the checkout desk.

> *Why do we think God has to fix our imperfections before we can enjoy eternity with him in heaven?*

"Oh, you might want to keep this one," the receptionist said with a smile, returning one of my coins. "This one is very valuable. See this flaw? I am a currency collector. I'm not sure exactly what it is worth, but I know it is worth a lot more than face value."

It seems rather strange that a society would highly value a coin because of a man-made flaw and devalue people because of God-allowed flaws.

"Keep it," I said, "It is worth more to you than it would be to me."

Yesterday, I would have kept it.

Listen
Read Psalm 139:13–14

Make a list of what you like, and don't like, about yourself. Circle dislikes that are within your power to change. Ask God to help you with the changes or acceptance.

- † Which list is longer? Which was easier?
- † As your day resumes, let God introduce you to the person He created you to be. (Spoiler alert: His lists are different.)
- † Can you discern a purpose for the "flaws" He has permitted?
- † Journal about the wonderful creation of **you** that God has revealed this day and night. Pray Psalm 139 over the person God is helping you become.

In Lieu Of

But Samuel replied: "Does the Lord delight in burnt offerings
and sacrifices as much as in obeying the Lord?
To obey is better than sacrifice, and to heed is better
than the fat of rams."

—1 Samuel 15:22

Sara had no delusions that a Bible study on the prophet Isaiah would be easy. But when frustration and confusion surfaced immediately with the first chapter, she was tempted to abandon it. The Israelites had forsaken God, so it was reasonable for God to send Isaiah to admonish them. But why did God contradict the laws in Exodus chapter 20 and throughout the book of Leviticus which demanded burnt offerings? Now, in Isaiah, He calls them detestable and says He finds no delight in them and does not even want them (Isaiah 1:11–20).

Already entangled in a web of uncertainty, Sara desperately needed firm reassurance that God was the same yesterday, today, and always. This study, however, appeared to have joined forces with the perplexity and confusion that engulfed her personal life as it unraveled a bit more each day. "Oh, Lord, help me," Sara prayed in defeat. Silence was her only answer.

Attempts to sleep were thwarted by an unceasing whirlwind of thoughts. Her marriage had not been a marriage for quite some time. A living arrangement, like college roommates without the fun, did not qualify as a marriage. However, tomorrow was their anniversary. Her dutiful husband would do what was expected. Flowers. Dinner. A boxed gift. Nice card. Then he would catch the news before crawling into bed.

For over a dozen years, they raised three children, finished college, and balanced career challenges. Their relationship was secure, dependable, efficient. But mostly, it was *there*, kinda like the refrigerator. Hypocritically, Sara resented the security his commitment promised. It failed to squelch the yearning ache in the pit of her stomach for a spark of passion in lieu of the most elegant bouquet or extravagant dinner. Maybe this was what God addressed through Isaiah.

> *How could I and God not want what we wanted?*

She tossed and turned as random thoughts continued to evolve around the confusion: "How could I and God not want what we wanted?" In her defense, Sara reasoned, God had commanded the sacrifices. She never asked for the flowers and dinner. Yet, it seemed to Sara there was a contradiction: God no longer wanted the sacrifices He had commanded. And she no longer wanted the flowers that expressed commitment instead of love.

Whether by blessing or exhaustion, sleep finally prevailed because morning awakened her. "Happy Anniversary." And forty-five minutes later, after a shower, coffee, and bagel, he left for work. As the door closed, her thoughts resumed. "Yes, I know he loves me. But he also loves his tackle box and golf clubs. And a beautiful bouquet once a year is not enough to convince me he loves me any differently. Oh, when did I begin to despise the flowers, fancy jewelry, fancy cards, and candle-lit dinners?" Startled by the thought, a dormant desire stirred within Sara, like a smoldering ember that demanded to be reignited.

When did their fervent goodbye kisses dwindle to a quick peck at the door? Could this faint glow of dying embers be all that remained of the inferno of love that once blazed between them? When had their conversations become information relays about the kids, cars, and calendars along with angry outbursts like the words he flung at her when she least expected it? Is it any wonder that her sigh of relief when he walked through the door at the end of the day now escaped her lips when he left in the morning? Defeated, Sara slumped into a kitchen chair. Her eyes rested on the passage in Isaiah. Could these random thoughts be connected with God's message to the Israelites?

Admittedly, Sara shouldered some of the blame for the dysfunction in their marriage. When they first married, she was delighted to fix dinner for her husband. Now, it was one more task she *had* to do. When was passion replaced with duty? Why had no one noticed the exchange of striving to please each other and overlook petty faults with mutual tolerance?

Momentarily awakened, the embers of hope were already fading, destined for eternal extinction in lieu of the passion they desired. God sent Isaiah to awaken Israel's passion for God. Who would be an Isaiah to spark the embers of their dying marriage?

"Oh, Lord!" she prayed, "Can You rekindle our marriage? Yes, I know You can. Show me the way. If what James 2:17 says is true—that faith without action is dead—then love without action must be dead, too. And action without love is also dead. Without passion, love dies. Oh, Lord, help me. Help us."

> *Without passion, love dies.*

Yes, their marriage was intact. But like the flowers, whose essence quickly withered, it felt worthless. We are relational beings, created for passion. Without passion, the gift of flowers, romantic dinners, and burnt offerings become nothing more than duty. And duty in lieu of passion honors no one.

Duty is a checklist. Duty drains joy from the sacrifice like the air from a balloon, leaving it empty and useless. Passion had once infused their joy, encouraging each to be a better person. Was it possible to reignite it? If so, how?

Her thoughts drifted to their wedding day. They had chosen as part of their vows 1 Corinthians 13, affectionately known as the love chapter. Paul said that even if we spoke in tongues, had the gift of prophecy, could fathom mysteries, were knowledgeable in all things, had faith to move mountains, or gave all our possession to the poor, without love, we gain nothing. It would be like a resounding gong or clanging cymbal (1 Corinthians 13:1–3). The pastor had reminded them that love is not just a feeling. Love is also a verb and verbs are action. But if the sacrifices, flowers, and dinner were the actions addressed, why did they feel like empty clanging gongs?

Sara turned to Mark chapter twelve where Jesus praised a teacher of the law who had responded that loving God and our neighbor is "more important than all burnt offerings and sacrifices" (Mark 12:33 NIV). Sara didn't want her husband going through the motions in lieu of passionate love any more than God wanted the Israelites going through the motions with the burnt offerings and sacrifices.

Suddenly, Paul's words illuminated the contradiction of what the law demanded, and God wanted. Love without action is worthless. Action without love is worthless. Sara wanted the flowers and dinner to celebrate their passionate love, just like God wants the passionate love represented in our burnt offerings. Action without passionate love is duty. And duty without passion cannot honor God any more than it can honor a marriage, however committed it is.

With new insight, Sara saw that the Lord clarifies what He wants in the first chapter of Isaiah. "I have more than enough of burnt offerings, of rams and the fat of fattened animals; I have no pleasure in the blood of bulls and lambs and goats. Stop bringing meaningless offerings! Your incense is detestable to me. Stop doing wrong. Learn to do right" (Isaiah 1:11, 13, 16–17). God never changed his mind. He merely articulated his original command. The *contradiction* started to make sense to Sara. There was no contradiction.

In lieu of passion, flowers and dinner might celebrate an anniversary, but not a marriage. God despised the burnt offerings just as Sara despised the flowers and dinner. When passion is reduced to duty, it honors no one except a date on the calendar. A fatted calf slapped on the altar might fulfill the law, but it fails to honor God unless it is done with passion, love, and gratitude.

> *When passion is reduced to duty, it honors no one except a date on the calendar.*

God commands sacrifice of our time, money, and service, not because He needs these things, not for us to be duty-bound, but to provide an opportunity for us to express our love, passion, and gratitude towards Him. Isaiah brought hope to the Israelites. Sara needed that hope in her marriage. Did she need it in her relationship with God as well?

Restoration begins with an honest assessment of the current condition and a commitment towards a desired outcome. Once Sara acknowledged her responsibility in the demise of their marriage, she became aware of the deterioration of her relationship with God. An avalanche of verses memorized from childhood formed a desperate prayer:

Create in me a pure heart, O God, and renew a steadfast spirit within me. Restore to me the joy of your salvation and grant me a willing spirit. Lord, I fear that my passion has dwindled to duty, and I no longer worship you with gladness nor come before you with joy-filled songs. Rekindle my passion for you so that You can take delight in my offerings. My love for You has not failed, but my passion is all but gone. Renew my heart. Revive my marriage. Fan these fading embers back to life. Lord Jesus, hear my cry.

(Inspired by Psalm 51; Psalm 100).

When a campfire is reduced to a few faint embers struggling to stay alive, dry tinder and wood are not enough to bring it back to life. A piece of cardboard can fan the embers until they glow brighter and finally ignite the tinder. But how do you reignite a smoldering marriage or dying faith?

"Take delight in the Lord, and he will give you the desires of your heart" (Psalm 37:4). A fresh awareness of God's presence throughout her day became Sara's tinder. Christian friends and church attendance fueled the smoldering campfire. But it was the very breath of God that breathed new life into her heart with a burning desire for His Word. Could God breathe new life into a marriage whose embers no longer glowed, nor any warmth arose from the ashes?

> *Where do you begin when what is wrong far outweighs any memories of what was once good?*

Where do you begin when what is wrong far outweighs any memories of what was once good? Is blind-induced hopelessness impossible to overcome? Do you just admit defeat? Or give it a fighting chance?

Your first commitment is to admit you need help. Maybe even professional help. Just because first aid immobilizes a broken leg does not eliminate the need for a physician. When your DIY skills and knowledge reach their limit, you do not hesitate to seek advice. Why do we fail to apply that logic to marriage? Sara's campfire needed attention. Did it require tinder and fresh wood or a professional make-over?

Earlier in their marriage, a prayer, an apology, acknowledgment, or hug were powerful healers for superficial wounds inflicted from the challenges of daily living. They were beyond that simple fix. Sara bowed her head to pray, but her tears washed the unformed words from her lips.

In the silence, a simple line from a song arose. "O, Be Careful Little Eyes What You See."[1] A childhood song about protecting your eyes, ears, hands, feet, heart, and mind so your actions would always honor God. As a married woman, that song helped Sara fulfill a vow to protect her marriage with a commitment to purposely avoid any opportunity for Satan to cause her eyes to drift. Sara refused to bad-mouth her husband at work. She made it a point to never be alone with a male co-worker, especially on days when they left the house in a huff. She was aware of Satan's trap that would make another man seem more perfect, more attentive than the one with whom she vowed to love for better or worse. She did not want to be attracted to forbidden fruit, no matter how sour the grapes in her own basket. She had kept that vow.

It was like the sun burst through the clouds and flooded every thought with a reality check. "Oh, you must indeed be careful," the warmth spoke to her heart, "be careful what your little eyes see, not just in other men, *but in your husband*. You have become an expert at seeing his faults. What if you looked instead for his good and let the faults get caught in the cobwebs of your critical spirit? Is it possible to discover again the man you married? The man you promised to love for better or worse? Oh, little eyes, choose carefully what you see."

> *Be careful what your little eyes see, not just in other men, but in your husband.*

Sara's viewfinder adjustment did not happen overnight, but eventually she learned to appreciate and even love things that were once annoying. Generally, you see what you are looking for. Remember the series of books "Where's Waldo?"[2] At first, he is elusive, then he gets easier to spot. Finding good in her husband was as challenging as finding Waldo, but eventually Sara's eyes discovered multiple "Waldos" (good in her hubby). Be careful little eyes, for you see what you want to see. You see what you are looking for.

At a time when she desperately needed reassurance, an ancient prophet named Isaiah stumbled into Sara's kitchen with a song from childhood. The encounter awakened her love for the Lord and her husband. Out of smoldering ashes, God breathed new life into a weary marriage and reignited her passion for God. Now each day was a celebration—in lieu of a few dates on the calendar.

Listen
Read Luke 6:42

We choose what we look for. Our "Waldos" can be positive or negative, strengths or flaws, opportunities or obstacles. It is your viewfinder. It is your choice.

✝ What do you tend to look for in others? Yourself? God? Circumstances?

✝ As your day resumes, be aware of your initial reaction to people and events.

✝ Does your Waldo-finder need adjustment? Purposely look for the good.

✝ Journal what your little eyes have seen this day and night. Create your Waldo list.

Pearly Wisdom

I have told you these things, so that in me you may have peace.
In this world you will have trouble. But take heart!
I have overcome the world.

—John 16:33

S himmering in iridescent luster with a soft inner glow that is unrivalled even among the most glorious gems of the world, the pearl's grandeur originates from an uninvited irritation. Some gems, such as diamonds, rubies, and sapphires, must be cut and polished to bring forth their beauty. Pearls are given to the world complete, perfect, exquisitely finished.

Natural pearls begin when a foreign object, usually a parasite, becomes lodged between an oyster's shell and its mantle.[1] The mantle is the thin layer of tissue separating the shell from the soft inner body. This tiny intruder becomes a source of irritation for the oyster. Usually, its efforts to expel it fail, triggering defensive secretions of a smooth, hard crystalline substance called *nacre* to surround the irritation, thus isolating the nuisance. As long as the irritation remains, the oyster continues secreting nacre until it is coated with multiple silky crystalline layers. The result is an ever-growing pearl. Generally, five years is required for a natural 3 mm pearl, although some cultured pearls require only a year before harvesting.

While nacre enables the oyster to deal with an irritation, its main purpose is forming the mother-of-pearl lining of the inner shell. The pearl's composite layers of microscopic crystals of calcium carbonate align perfectly with one another. The result reflects and refracts light that interacts with layers of crystals creating the distinctive iridescent rainbow of light and color found only in pearls. Wild pearls are extremely rare and quite valuable, so most of the pearls on the market are cultured. This means humans, not nature, introduce the irritation. But since only the oyster or its mollusk cousins can produce the layers of nacre, every pearl, whether wild or cultured, is considered a natural pearl. X-rays can determine culturally introduced irritants.

God enables oysters to cope with an annoyance via a process which completely encompasses the irritant until only the valuable gem is visible. If God uniquely synchronizes an oyster with an irritation to produce a magnificent pearl, imagine what He can do with irritations in the lives of those who are created in His own image and likeness (Genesis 1:26).

Imagine His light shining through layers of grace-nacre.

When God allows challenges and irritations in our lives, He also provides layers of grace, so we do not simply cope, but triumph. Imagine His light shining through layers of grace-nacre, so the world no longer sees you or your irritant but only God's shimmering grace surrounding you.

Jesus promises in John 16:33, "In this world you will have trouble. But take heart! I have overcome the world." While on this earth, we may not always understand why God allows irritations in our lives, but we can trust His plan for us to be gems that bring Him glory. When we pray "Your will be done" from the Lord's Prayer (Matthew 6:10), we declare our trust in God to provide the grace-nacre we need to triumph over life's annoyances.

In the garden, Jesus prayed that same prayer (Luke 22:42) before He faced a far worse irritant than we will ever encounter.

But Hebrews 12:2 says, "For the joy set before him he endured the cross, scorning its shame." That joy was us: a priceless gem.

Imagine your joy as you stand before our heavenly Father to lay your crown embedded with pearls before His throne (Revelation 4:10). A crown of shimmering pearls of God-endorsed irritations surrounded by grace-nacre reflecting and refracting His glorious radiance not just on this earth, but for all eternity!

The Pearly Gates:
An Interesting Vision of Heaven

The apostle John describes heaven in Revelation chapter 21. The walls and foundation were twelve layers of gems. Imagine the beauty of being surrounded by walls of jasper, sapphire, agate, emerald, onyx, ruby, chrysolite, beryl, topaz, turquoise, jacinth, and amethyst. "The twelve gates were twelve pearls, each gate made of a single pearl." The streets are made of gold, "as pure as transparent glass." There was no need of the sun or moon to shine on it, for the glory of God gives it light (See Revelation 21:18–23).

Walls of sparkling gems would be wonderful enough, but even more amazing is that God chose twelve grand pearls for the gates. Twelve iridescent pearl gates shimmering in the luster of grace-covered irritations reflecting and refracting the glory of God. What a thought. What a sight. What an incredible plan. We are almost encouraged to pray for irritations just so we can present pearls of glory to our Lord and King when we walk through those pearly gates. Well, almost.

Listen

Read 2 Corinthians 4:15

We all have irritations. But when your irritations are surrounded with grace-nacre, people will give God honor and praise. Remember, pearls take time.

✝ List some of your irritations. Draw circles around each annoyance as a visual of grace-nacre.

✝ As you resume your day, sprinkle grace-nacre on your daily irritations.

✝ If hurtful words threaten to spill out, capture them with nacre.

✝ If hurtful words escaped your lips, administer a shot of nacre to yourself.

✝ Journal your pearls this day and night—those encased and those still being formed.

Sin's Delightful Appeal

I have hidden your word in my heart,
that I might not sin against you.

—Psalm 119:11 (NLT)

The chorus of children's laughter drifted from the barn and harmonized with the calves, chickens, and lambs. "Oh, they must have found the kittens," Suzy interrupted, "I wondered if Kally Kat would bring her brood out with all that extra kid-energy around."

It had been a perfect day. On the open porch, the sisters savored lilacs, birds, and iced tea. They relished a welcome dose of adult conversation. The sprawling homestead kept the cousins occupied within sight without being underfoot. After a lifetime of opposition over sports, boys, career paths, sushi, and music, motherhood solidified their friendship. They fiercely guarded any time together.

Finally, the irresistible peal of excitement lassoed their hearts. "Aww, come on!" Suzy abandoned their plans for solitude. "Let's join 'em. Talk can wait. Kittens cannot."

Quietly they approached the excited cluster of tousled heads. What they saw startled them. "Run! Run for the house! Quick!

Go. Go. Go." Suzy shouted the alarm. Obediently, they bolted for the house, but not before each child snatched up a tiny black and white wiggly fur ball.

Baby skunks are cute. They have no natural fear of humans. These curious, docile creatures, if handled from birth, make playful, affectionate pets. They can even be litter box trained. Their infamous scent glands are not activated until several weeks after birth and can be surgically removed. Newborn skunks love to snuggle inside your shirt, unseen, protected, and close to your heart. However, when forced to stay secluded, they scratch and bite demanding freedom to investigate the world on their own terms.

With no intended disrespect, sin is quite similar to these adorable little black and white critters. Rarely is sin presented as offensive. At least not at first. We are as naturally repulsed by raw evil as we are by the smell of an adult skunk.

> *Like a baby skunk tucked inside your shirt, initially sin's hidden presence is comforting, warm, charming, and even enchanting.*

Sin can be delightfully appealing with elements of playfulness and curiosity to camouflage the stench of evil concealed just beyond our senses. Like a baby skunk tucked inside your shirt, initially sin's hidden presence is comforting, warm, charming, and even enchanting. You might be the only one aware of what is happening close to your heart as you struggle to keep your little sin a secret. You deny its existence for fear others will think less of you. Even when sin wrestles to emerge, you can successfully keep the scratching and biting hidden. Yet, you are fully aware of the battle raging inside your shirt, demanding its own way.

Your secret will not stay secret for long. Once a baby skunk matures, its scent glands likewise mature, emitting a distinctive telltale odor easily identifiable even at a distance. That is a skunk's primary defensive weapon and administered only when an intruder ignores the warning "dance." One shot is usually enough to discourage further conflict without administering serious injury, except to sting the eyes. However, its oily stench lingers. Once a person or dog endures the spray, it does not take long for them to become desensitized to the offensive odor—an achievement not appreciated by those close by.

Sin has a similar effect on us. Initially, sin can be delightfully appealing. We tuck it close to our heart, embrace its secret ambiance, ignore the scratches on our conscience, and deny the stench we once found offensive. But just as you can only hide a skunk inside your shirt for a limited time, sin eventually makes its presence known. Sin's stench is offensive to everyone except those who have acclimated to its odor. Sin prefers the company of those who do not call sin, sin. Therefore, once we admit sin stinks, we must remove ourselves from it.

> *Sin's stench is offensive to everyone except those who have acclimated to its odor.*

Once the skunk is removed from your shirt, the stench remains. A solution of white vinegar, 3% hydrogen peroxide, and baking soda mixed with Dawn® dishwashing detergent dissolves and removes the skunk odor-causing oils instead of just spreading them.

But how do you remove the stench of sin? David said, "If I had not confessed the sin in my heart, the Lord would not have listened" (Psalm 66:18 NLT). Confession exposes the sin, but only one solution removes its stench and stain: the blood of Christ. Titus 3:5 says, "He saved us, not because of the righteous things we had done, but because of his mercy. He washed away our sins, giving us a new birth and new life through the Holy Spirit" (NLT).

Prevention is essential with skunks. Stay away from their habitat. If you do encounter one, flee. Solomon gave the same warning about sin as represented by an adulterous woman. "Keep to a path far from her, do not go near the door of her house" (Proverbs 5:8).

Baby skunks have the potential to become delightful companions. But sin never will. Regular time in God's Word will protect you from sin's delightful appeal. It will also prevent you from becoming desensitized to sin's stench. "I have hidden your word in my heart, that I might not sin against you" (Psalm 119:11 NLT). Sin loses its appeal when you delight yourself in God's Word.

 *Listen*

Read Hebrews 3:12–13

Before you resume your day, tuck a cotton ball in your pocket to represent a cute little sin-skunk. Imagine its scent glands maturing, so everyone knows the secret-sin you think you are hiding.

† What odor would you give sin? (A lemon smells fresh until it gets moldy).

† Why are we immune to our sin-odor, yet so keen on someone else's?

† Use Psalm 119:11 to personalize a prayer for sin prevention.

† Journal whatever God has revealed to you this day and night.

You can find some solutions to de-skunk your dog in **Listen for More**, page 235.

LISTEN FOR HIS VOICE

My Lump of Coal

Oh, the simple joy of deceitful sin.
We embrace its lies. Deny its lethal sting.
Tightly I hold my burning lump of coal.
As it singes my hand, blistering my soul.

There is no reason for Jesus to add
those three little words. They just make me mad.
"Forgive me, Lord" should be prayer enough.
"As I forgive" is unnecessary stuff.

Shrewdly, sin can justify my grudge.
Prosecuting attorney. Jury and Judge.
Why add "as I forgive" to the equation?
It is not required for my salvation.

This smoldering coal nestled in my palm
possesses no power to right a wrong.
Still, I clutch it tight as deeper it burns.
Without satisfaction, without a concern.

And what is even more infuriating:
The more it burns, the less they are caring.
My grip I release. My sin I confess.
I reach for You, Lord, and Your forgiveness.

It may take some time for my wounds to heal.
Lord, fill me with peace that no one can steal.
May these scars on my hands serve to remind me
what Your nail-scarred hands did on Calvary.

"Father forgive them. They know not what they do."
That is forgiveness that is honest and true.
Lord, help me let go of sin's mighty grip.
And reach for Your hand and let my coal slip.

Father forgive me as I forgive others.
For are they not my sisters and brothers?

Some Coal-Releasing Remedies

And forgive us our sins, as we have forgiven those who sin against us.

—Matthew 6:12 NLT

Jesus said, "Father, forgive them, for they do not know what they are doing."

—Luke 23:34

Dear friends, never take revenge.
Leave that to the righteous anger of God.
For the Scriptures say, "I will take revenge; I will pay them back," says the Lord.
Instead, "If your enemies are hungry, feed them.
If they are thirsty, give them something to drink.
In doing this, you will heap burning coals of shame on their heads."

—Romans 12:19–20 NLT

But Joseph said to them, "Don't be afraid. Am I in the place of God?
You intended to harm me, but God intended it for good to accomplish what is now being done, the saving of many lives.

—Genesis 50:19–20

Do not repay evil with evil or insult with insult.
On the contrary, repay evil with blessing,
because to this you were called so that you may inherit a blessing.

—1 Peter 3:9

Listen

Read Ephesians 4:31–32

Press a jagged rock into your palm to represent your lump of coal. Envision it smoldering within your fist. Give Jesus permission to reveal any unforgiveness—even if self-inflicted.

+ Prayerfully choose one or two of the coal-releasing remedies listed above.

+ As your day resumes, let God's love engulf your lump of coal. Deep burns take time to heal.

+ Journal what God has revealed to you this day and night. Write a prayer of gratitude or a plea for help. It is okay to pray while you feel angry, hurt, frustrated, or helpless in your situation. Jesus understands and has the scars to prove it.

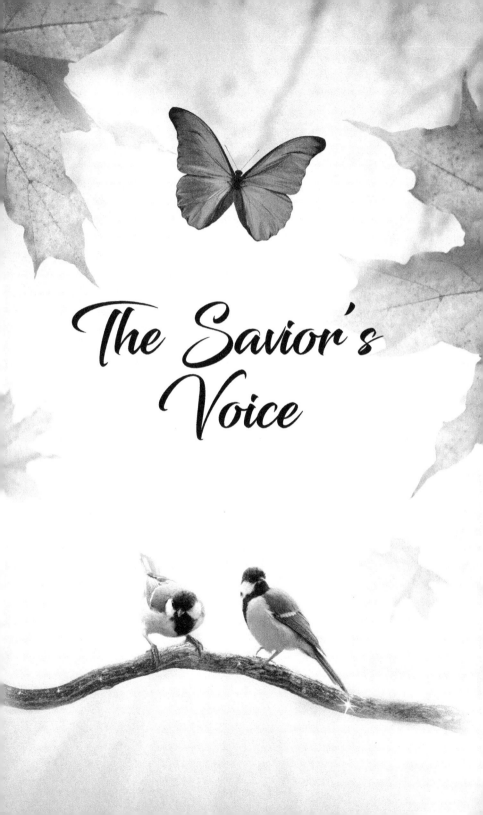

The Savior's Voice

Lost. Found. Home.

*If you declare with your mouth, "Jesus is Lord," and
believe in your heart that God raised him from the dead,
you will be saved.*

—Romans 10:9

The poster displayed the heart-tugging picture of someone's missing pet. "Lost dog. Reward, Beloved child's pet. Last seen . . . Please call . . ."

Have you known that helpless feeling when your dog or cat is lost? Have you felt the emptiness in the pit of your stomach as your calls echo back unanswered? Have you fought hopelessness when the frantic search yields nothing?

While all that drama is unfolding, chances are whoever is lost is happily pursuing a bunny trail of some sort, frolicking with a newfound friend, or taking a nap in a cozy spot. You are in a panic. Yet the one you are looking for does not even realize they are lost!

Have you ever gotten lost driving to a destination? How many miles does it take before you realize you are lost? How many more miles before asking for directions? For some drivers, it does not matter if you are lost as long as you are making good time. The truth is: you were lost as soon as you missed the first turn. Lost does not feel like lost until you have been lost enough to realize it.

Spiritually, we can be lost even while attending church, serving the poor, or raising children with good manners. Lost is just lost.

Even as it grazed within the flock, the lost sheep was lost. Since it did not wander back on its own, there is a good chance the Good Shepherd found it before it even knew it was lost (Luke 15:4–7).

Using the analogy of the Good Shepherd, how are you living as God's sheep? Are you close to the Shepherd? Are you on the outside, wondering what it would be like to be in His flock? Are you in His flock, but hanging out in the outer fringe so you can occasionally frolic in the thicket? Are you close to the Shepherd, but have strayed just beyond the sound of His voice? Realizing that you are lost is the beginning of *found*.

> *Realizing that you are lost is the beginning of* found.

The Good News is, once you realize you are lost, found is possible. You might remember Will Rogers's iconic proverb, "If you find yourself in a hole, the first thing to do is stop digging."[1] Well, when you realize you are lost, the first thing you need to do is stop going in the wrong direction. The technical word is *repent* which means to" turn around" or to "change one's mind."

The Good News is you never lost the Shepherd's love. Scripture is clear. "For I am convinced that neither death nor life, neither angels nor demons, neither the present nor the future, nor any powers, neither height nor depth, nor anything else in all creation, will be able to separate us from the love of God that is in Christ Jesus our Lord" (Romans 8:38–39). God loves you. Lost or found. Saved or not. Hopeless or hope-filled. God's love is unconditional. He cannot love you more. And He cannot love you less.

Jesus waits for you to invite Him into your life. "Behold, I stand at the door and knock. If anyone hears My voice and opens the door, I will come in to him and dine with him, and he with Me" (Revelation 3:20 NKJV). Opening that door is your decision.

Your sin is not news to the One who knows everything. "All have sinned and fall short of the glory of God" (Romans 3:23). Sadly, "the wages of sin is death" (Romans 6:23).

Jesus will not take your sin from you. Just as He waits for you to invite Him into your life, He waits for you to confess (give) your sin to Him so it can be nailed to the cross of Salvation.

The invitation for an eternity with Him in heaven is available once you meet the requirements. Heaven is holy, with no sin. And no sin is allowed to enter. Therefore, in order to enter, you need to be holy, pure, and blameless. But what does that mean?

If you had a glass of pure water and put one drop of sewage in it, it would no longer be pure. If you add more pure water, it would be diluted, but still not pure. No amount of pure water will purify it. That glass of water is your life. The sewage is sin. The added water is good works. No matter how small and insignificant the sin; no matter how much water (good deeds) are added, you will never be pure enough to get into heaven. On your own, you will never qualify for an eternity in heaven.

> *On your own, you will never qualify for an eternity in heaven.*

Thankfully, Jesus can accomplish what good intentions cannot. Imagine, if you will, giving your glass of sewer water to Jesus and receiving, instead, His glass of pure Living Water. His life. His purity. Himself. Imagine being holy, pure, and blameless in God's sight. Imagine being clothed in His righteousness (Isaiah 61:10; Ephesians 1:4).

The thing is, we will know Jesus as Lord whether we accept His invitation or not. Philippians 2:10–11 says that "every knee should bow . . . and every tongue acknowledge that Jesus Christ is Lord." That means that everyone will know throughout eternity. There is no default setting on eternity. Whether we accept the invitation or reject it, *everyone will know Jesus is Lord.* Whether eternity is in heaven or hell, we will know.

When you invite Jesus to be Lord *of* your life, rather than just Lord *in* your life, He "is able to do immeasurably more than all we ask or imagine, according to his power that is at work within us" (Ephesians 3:20).

Tired of being lost? Allow Jesus to find you, wrap His arms around you, and take you home. If you want to make that decision today so that you are not lost for eternity, or if you want to rededicate your life, you can pray this prayer. It is as simple as ABC: **Admit. Believe. Confess.**

> *We will know Jesus as Lord whether we accept His invitation or not.*

Lord Jesus, I am tired of being lost. I admit I am a sinner. I admit I have strayed. I invite You into my life. I give to You my sin-filled life in exchange for Your righteousness. Thank You for what You did for me on Calvary so that I can enjoy eternal life with You in heaven. I invite You to be Lord of my life, not just Lord in my life. Work in me and through me so that others will see my deeds but glorify You. Fill me with joy in Your presence—here on this earth and for all eternity. I was a lost sheep, but now I am found in my Shepherd's arms. Safe. Secure. Home.

My Dear Reader,

If you prayed that prayer, tell someone. Share the Good News of your salvation. Did you know that the angels rejoice whenever a sinner repents? (Luke 15:10). Do you know that you just experienced something the angels long to understand? (1 Peter 1:10–12). If you feel sheepish about returning to His flock, please know that there is more rejoicing in heaven over one lost sinner who repents and returns to God than over ninety-nine righteous followers who have not strayed (Luke 15:7).

Indeed, this is a glorious day! Do you know that your name is written in the Book of Life? (Revelation 13:8). The Book of Life is the admission roster for heaven. You will not just be admitted, you will be home. Jesus promises in John 14:2–3 that He has prepared a place for you. Congratulations! And welcome to the family. I am proud of you! If you have a moment, I would love to hear about it. Please email me at marietpalecek@gmail.com or visit my website at www.marietpalecek.com.

Praise the Lord.

Affectionately,

Marie T. Palecek

If you declare with your mouth, "Jesus is Lord," and believe in your heart that God raised him from the dead, you will be saved.—Romans 10:9

For it is by grace you have been saved, through faith—and this is not from yourselves, it is the gift of God—not by works, so that no one can boast.—Ephesians 2:8–9

All who are victorious will be clothed in white. I will never erase their names from the Book of Life, but I will announce before my Father and his angels that they are mine.

—Revelation 3:5 (NLT)

Listen
Read 1 John 4:19

Sometimes, your decision to follow Jesus feels like it is yours alone. And it is. But do you realize how relentlessly God pursues your heart? Can you fathom how much He loves you?

Listen to "Reckless Love" (Live with story) by Cory Asbury, *Heaven Come 2017* via YouTube.[2] Let these twelve minutes minister to your soul. Imagine God's warm hug and immense joy.

✝ What is your initial reaction to this song and message?

✝ Reflect on the person you were while God relentlessly pursued your heart.

✝ As your day resumes, invite God to remind you of His presence and His relentless love.

✝ Journal what God has revealed this day and night about His relentless love for you.

Salvation's Chrysalis

Therefore, if anyone is in Christ, he is a new creation;
old things have passed away;
behold, all things have become new.

—2 Corinthians 5:17 (NKJV)

Meltdowns usually conjure images of defiant toddlers wreaking havoc in the checkout line or of the desperate mother at the end of her tolerance rope. Or maybe, a cantankerous clerk who reached the limit on equally cantankerous customers. The thesaurus produces a cascade of negative synonyms for meltdown: collapse, breakdown, failure, disaster, ruins, and destruction. However, not all meltdowns are destructive.

Melted plastic can be poured into molds to produce new useful products. Another example is waterproof, wind-resistant fire starters created with wax, egg cartons, and wood shavings. The combined combustible materials become more efficient than each is individually. While these meltdowns produce new products, they are the same materials, just restructured.

Complete meltdowns dramatically transform one thing into something entirely new. Fluttering around our yards are prime examples of dramatic, complete meltdowns. Within the seemingly delicate chrysalis, a caterpillar undergoes an amazing transformation—a complete meltdown—before it emerges as a butterfly.[1]

Caterpillars reduce their entire being into *imaginal* cells, which, like stem cells, can become any type of cell. This process is called holometabolism (*holo* meaning "total") plus (*metabolous* meaning "change"). Total change.

Inside the chrysalis, the caterpillar liquefies. These imaginal cells put themselves back together into an entirely new creation, with a new shape, new abilities, new desires, and a new purpose. A caterpillar's main agenda consists of crawling around, gnawing on leaves while eluding being eaten. Butterflies flutter from flower to flower, sip its sweet nectar, and strive to fulfill a far greater purpose: reproduction.

Caterpillars are bugs, self-serving destructive creepy bugs. Butterflies symbolize hope. Butterflies grace gift cards, jewelry, purses, clothes, and even the pages of this book as a source of inspiration and encouragement; a status caterpillars will forever lack.

Caterpillars are self-focused: What can I eat? Who might eat me? There is no space in the caterpillar's brain to contemplate a purpose beyond the immediate. They have no desire for sweet nectar or fluttering or providing for future generations.

> Yet the caterpillar willingly surrenders to the chrysalis.

Yet the caterpillar willingly surrenders to the chrysalis. It undergoes a complete meltdown within its delicate shell to emerge as an entirely new creation with new abilities, desires, perspective, and a new purpose.

Christians undergo a dramatic transformation that is no less miraculous. While some dramatic meltdowns are beneficial, spiritual meltdowns are essential. Paul confirmed this in 2 Corinthians 5:17. "Therefore, if anyone is in Christ, he is a new creation; old things have passed away; behold, all things have become new" (NKJV).

Sin no longer overpowers us. We are overcomers, even over sinful desires.

Susan explained her experience this way: "Before accepting Christ, my life revolved around soap operas. While I never endorsed the ungodly choices on the screen, I sometimes wondered if this form of entertainment was wrong. I prayed about it. I felt no prompting to quit. However, I soon realized their hold on me had lifted. It was not until they were no longer enjoyable that I realized God's transforming power was indeed at work in me."

Accepting Christ as our Lord and Savior alters our eternal life. But it also enables us to gain a new perspective on our earthly life. Things, which seemed important, begin to lose their grip compared to what is eternal. Paul accurately expressed this to the Philippians.

But whatever were gains to me I now consider loss for the sake of Christ. What is more, I consider everything a loss because of the surpassing worth of knowing Christ Jesus my Lord, for whose sake I have lost all things. I consider them garbage, that I may gain Christ and be found in him.

—Philippians 3:7–9

As soon as we accept God's gift of salvation, our total meltdown begins. Within the chrysalis of salvation, we become a new creation. Our purpose shifts from self-gratification to God-honoring deeds. Uncharacteristically, we desire to share the Gospel, reach the lost, serve the homeless, attend church, and intentionally make time to study His Word.

Without God's Spirit alive and active within us, natural human desires run contrary to God's purpose. We simply cannot love the unlovable, forgive the unforgivable, and desire to reach the unreachable. Yet as Christians, we can accomplish these impossible tasks with gusto! "Very truly I tell you, whoever believes in me will do the works I have been doing, and they will do even greater things than these" (John 14:12). Those are not the words of John, Paul, or Peter. That inconceivable promise comes from Jesus.

> *Within salvation's chrysalis, God miraculously transforms our desires, perception, and purpose into a new creation.*

Within salvation's chrysalis, God miraculously transforms our desires, perception, and purpose into a new creation that can do in Christ beyond any ability or desire we might have on our own. Unlike the butterfly, whose beauty fades, we continue to be "transformed into his image with ever-increasing glory, which comes from the Lord, who is the Spirit" (2 Corinthians 3:18). Our transformation continues with "ever-increasing glory." That is an incredible thought.

Before gaining a lofty perspective, before considering anything beyond its immediate needs, and before accumulating frequent flyer miles fluttering on delicate wings, the caterpillar must surrender to the chrysalis as a bug. A caterpillar cannot begin to think like a butterfly until after the transformation is complete.

Likewise, our transformation requires a willing step in faith to accept God's gift of salvation. Before we clean up our act, and before we have all the answers, we must step into salvation's chrysalis as a sinner-bug. Then, once within the chrysalis's embrace, our miraculous meltdown begins until we emerge like a butterfly. A new creation. We leave behind our old life to flutter forth with new desires to fulfill God's will, to sip the sweetness of God's goodness, to dance, inspire, and encourage.

Our "Christian chrysalis" is symbolized by baptism. "For you were buried with Christ when you were baptized. And with him you were raised to new life because you trusted the mighty power of God, who raised Christ from the dead" (Colossians 2:12 NLT).

Caterpillars and butterflies have different perspectives of the world, different ambitions, different purposes. "The old life is gone; a new life has begun!" (2 Corinthians 5:17 NLT). An exciting God-centered, hope-filled, inspiring life awaits the butterfly in you as a new creation.

Look up Galatians 5:22-23. List the nine fruits of the Spirit:

1. ....

2. ....

3. ....

4. ....

5. ....

6. ....

7. ....

8. ....

9. ....

Listen

Read 2 Corinthians 5:17 and Galatians 5:22–23

Caterpillars do not instantly morph into butterflies. We should not expect our sinner-bug selves to emerge as butterflies overnight either. Give yourself time. Let the Holy Spirit work in you.

✝ How would you define your life as a sinner-bug?

✝ How evident are the fruits of the Spirit (Galatians 5:22–23) in your thoughts, words, actions, desires, purpose, or viewpoint?

✝ Resume this day with fresh appreciation and awareness of God's Spirit at work in you, around you, and through you.

✝ Journal your gratitude, commitment, or desires. Ask for forgiveness, courage, perseverance, strength, or hope.

Want to make waterproof, wind-resistant fire starters? Instructions are in **Listen for More**, page 237.

Broken

My sacrifice, O God, is a broken spirit; a broken and
contrite heart, you, God, will not despise.

—Psalm 51:17

My favorite garden tool is broken. Not "Oh no, I broke my favorite garden tool." But rather, it wasn't my favorite until it was broken.

A hand cultivator is a three-prong garden tool that fits in your palm. It is lightweight but sturdy, and when used as intended, does an excellent job to loosen up the soil. Force it to endure abuse beyond the strength of its welds and eventually the two outer prongs snap! Hallelujah. You are left holding a single prong wonder tool, surpassing any tool in your shed.

Stripped of its hindering outer prongs, the remaining center prong becomes an extension of your hand. It has strength to lift buried timbers or release boulders wedged deep within the earth's crust. It effortlessly navigates with efficiency around plants to loosen soil, swipe weed seedlings, and uproot established weeds without being disruptive. It administers precision transplantation for delicate seedlings.

Brokenness transforms a simple hand cultivator into an indispensable garden tool, single-handedly accomplishing far more than its original cumbersome design. And unlike the three-prong edition, it will never spring up from the ground when stepped on or stab your foot accidentally.

In life, brokenness hurts. Yet God accomplishes in the heart of the brokenhearted something that far exceeds anything achievable prior to being broken. Psalm 51:17 says, "My sacrifice, O God, is a broken spirit; a broken and contrite heart you, God, will not despise."

> God's plan will never take us where His power cannot reach us.

There is a hope that is only experienced via brokenness. Christian hope is a sure thing. We do not know how. We do not know when. We do not know what. But we do know God's plan will never take us where His power cannot reach us. That is hope.

While I cherish the efficiency of my broken garden tool, in real life, even fools do not welcome brokenness. Whenever possible, we seek to avoid the pain of unfulfilled dreams and people who let us down. We gladly forfeit familiarity with the hopelessness of desperate pleas that seem to fall on deaf ears and echo through the emptiness of a shattered heart. We prefer to skip the labor pains and just embrace the birth. We want to forego the rigorous climb and the daily struggles and just sign up instead for a Norman Rockwell snapshot of a blessed life.

Let's face it. Proclaiming "God is good" is easier when life is good. Pain and loss are more acceptable on someone else's Facebook page. Sincerely saying, "I will pray for you" is greatly preferred over needing someone's prayers. We prefer brokenness, like a garden tool, to be at arm's length.

Until broken, a cultivator remains a cultivator, not an indispensable tool. The brokenness in ourselves that we try to avoid is the very tool God uses to minister to others. However, God has no desire to break our spirit. His plan is for us to prosper with hope and a future (Jeremiah 29:11) as an extension of His hand. By the way, that promise in Jeremiah occurred after the prophet informed the Israelites that they would endure seventy years of brokenness (Jeremiah 29:4–10).

Alcoholics Anonymous[1] founder, William Griffith Wilson, better known as Bill W., understood the brokenness of alcoholism. That brokenness inspired the foundation of Alcoholics Anonymous in 1934. Alcoholics are best equipped to help others get on the road to recovery. Similarly, cancer support groups do not wonder what a newly diagnosed person is going through. They know because they've been there.

Sometimes we think we understand. Take the mother of three who underwent an emergency hysterectomy. She consoled her friend struggling with infertility with, "I know exactly how you feel; I cannot have any more children either." No. She does not know exactly how it feels. She cannot. She only knows how it feels not to be able to have any *more* children. It is not the same.

Thankfully, empathy does not require full understanding of the depth of someone's pain to offer comfort. Often, doctors and nurses make the worst patients. But patients can become compassionate doctors and nurses beyond a medical degree because they understand a patient's needs.

Broken and contrite spirits are better equipped to minister to spirits that are broken. Their strength and gentleness effectively offer understanding, comfort, and hope. That is because their brokenness helps them to be more aware of God's presence in their life. They do not worry about what "the future holds, because they know who holds the future."[2] That is

> *Broken and contrite spirits are better equipped to minister to spirits that are broken.*

hope. Not just hope for the brokenhearted, but the hope *of* the brokenhearted. Our God is an awesome God! He rejoices in what He can do through our brokenness when all we feel is broken.

Romans 8:28 is overused and often misquoted, yet it still rings with truth. "And we know that in all things God works for the good of those who love him, who have been called according to his purpose."

Life is not always fair. Sometimes evil seems to have the upper hand. Good people get hurt. Things that should not happen, happen. Yet in all of it, we can be confident God's purpose is always for our good. It is an amazing blessing when our brokenness becomes one of God's favorite tools for accomplishing His will. Brokenhearted people instinctively understand what others simply cannot.

People are not perfect. Our world is far from perfect. We contend with sunken timbers, embedded boulders, and pervasive sin-weeds wreaking havoc on our peaceful landscape. In this broken world, our natural self, like the cultivator, has outer prongs such as pride and self-reliance, which hinder our effectiveness to uproot, dislodge, and fix sin's destructive effects until one day something snaps! We are broken. Once pride and self-reliance lie useless, our Lord celebrates our brokenness. Without these hindering prongs, we become a powerful tool in the hands of the Master Gardener.

The Son of God became a man. A broken man. Jesus was broken *for us*. We become an extension of God's hand as He moves through us with confidence, precision, and ease, accomplishing far more than possible before our brokenness. God uses the things that bring us down to lift us up. And when He lifts us up, He enables us to lift others.

> *God uses the things that bring us down to lift us up. And when He lifts us up, He enables us to lift others.*

Paul understood what it felt like to be one of God's broken garden tools. In 2 Corinthians chapter 12, Paul speaks humbly of visions and revelations from the Lord:

If I wanted to boast, I would be no fool in doing so, because I would be telling the truth. But I won't do it, because I don't want anyone to give me credit beyond what they can see in my life or hear in my message, even though I have received such wonderful revelations from God. So, to keep me from becoming proud, I was given a thorn in my flesh, a messenger from Satan to torment me and keep me from becoming proud.

Three different times I begged the Lord to take it away. Each time he said, "My grace is all you need. My power works best in weakness." So now I am glad to boast about my weaknesses, so that the power of Christ can work through me. That's why I take pleasure in my weaknesses, and in the insults, hardships, persecutions, and troubles that I suffer for Christ. For when I am weak, then I am strong.

—2 Corinthians 12:6–10 (NLT)

God enabled Paul to find delight in his brokenness. Psalm 147:3 says "He heals the brokenhearted." Did you notice God does not fix the brokenhearted? He heals. God indeed loved Paul and He healed him, although not the way Paul requested. Paul was a cultivator with two hindering prongs. He admitted one was pride. Before Paul could become one of

The power of sin must be broken, so God can make us "perfect," strong in Him and effective in our ministry.

God's most oft-used tools, the weld had to be broken. The power of sin must be broken, so God can make us "perfect," strong in Him and effective in our ministry.

Are you one of God's oft-used tools? What prongs must be broken for you to become a more effective tool in God's hand? What brokenness has God allowed in your life that enables you to display His glory? Are you ready to celebrate brokenness so His glory can shine through your broken life?

We cannot embrace all God has prepared for us until we embrace our brokenness. Whatever I plan to accomplish in my garden, whatever the season or task, my most indispensable tool is broken. Likewise, I am eternally blessed each time I feel God's hand guide my brokenness to administer His hope, encouragement, cheer, assistance, forgiveness, challenge, or love to brokenhearted people like me. "The Spirit of the Sovereign Lord is upon me, for the Lord has anointed me to bring good news to the poor. He has sent me to comfort the brokenhearted" (Isaiah 61:1 NLT).

> We cannot embrace all God has prepared for us until we embrace our brokenness.

Listen
Read Psalm 34:18

God does not cause our brokenness. When He allows brokenness, He uses it. Before you journal this day, break a dinner roll or cracker to represent brokenness. Your brokenness and Jesus' brokenness.

✝ What brokenness has God allowed in your life?

✝ How has God used (or could use) your brokenness to minister to others?

✝ Throughout this day and night be aware of broken people. Let God use your brokenness to administer a smile or kind word.

✝ Journal where brokenness found you today. If your brokenness needs God's healing touch, give it to Him. A father cannot fix a broken toy if the child clutches it in their hands. Let go and let God.

If you thirst for an extended time in prayer, I have included a reflection called "Broken Communion" in **Listen for More**, page 239.

Rust to Restoration

He restores my soul.

—Psalm 23:3 (NKJV)

Spring's proclamations in Minnesota are not limited to bursting daffodils, cheerful robins, and the honk of returning geese. As winter surrenders to spring, a distinctive rumble joins the chorus as classic and restored street rods emerge to reclaim their prominence on Minnesota roadways.

These restored gems signify more than victory over cabin fever. They signify a victory over rust, decay, and time itself. Minnesotans' love affair with automobiles is legendary and could possibly predate Henry Ford's revolutionary assembly line, built on the shores of the Mississippi River in St. Paul circa 1925.

MSRA (Minnesota Street Rods Association) was established in 1967 and hosts Back to the Fifties each June. This three-day event carpets the Minnesota State Fairgrounds with over 12,000 vintage vehicles (manufactured prior to 1964) with more than a million spectators. It is one of the largest gatherings of car enthusiasts in the world, second only to NSRA (National Street Rod Association).

This annual event, however, is not enough to satisfy Minnesotans' vintage itch. Car enthusiasts gather across the state on any given weekend throughout summer and fall to share their love for metal, wheels, and bratwurst. One of the largest events is the Northern Lights Annual Pig Roast held in Hugo, Minnesota each

September with over 1,000 entries. The Pig Roast is for entrants. The cars are for everyone. Spectators enjoy seeing vintage machines in mint condition while their owners share stories of the ones that did not get away.

A few owners purchase their cars in show condition or hire a restoration team. However, the majority have dedicated hours upon passionate hours to bring new life to rusting chunks of metal. With their fresh paint job and pinstriping, it is hard to imagine the immeasurable investment required to reverse the brutality time and neglect had inflicted on rusting metal. But their owners proudly admit, "It was worth it."

To bring a car from rust to restoration requires knowledge, passion, time, and cost. Before embarking on any restoration project, whether it is an antique car or a piece of heirloom furniture, the first step is to determine whether it is worth it.

When King David said of the Good Shepherd, "He restores my soul" (Psalm 23:3), he confirmed God's ability to restore us, and also our worthiness of the restoration process. If we were not worth it, God would not undertake the restoration. We are worth the cost, the time, the effort. Let that sink in and minister to your soul. God says you are worth it.

> Mint condition has never been a requirement for Jesus to cherish us.

Any restoration project requires knowledge and vision. Street rod enthusiasts assess value in something most would consider worthless junk. They do not see the rusting shell of a Model A Ford huddled under decades of debris in grandfather's chicken coop. Instead, they envision a shiny red street rod with mag wheels and hear the deep rumbling of a fine-tuned engine. The ability to see the potential plus the desire and knowledge to see it fulfilled, is what makes these miraculous transformations possible. Have you ever felt like a worthless, rusted shell peering out from under a pile of "yuck"? I think we all have at one time or another.

Fortunately, mint condition has never been a requirement for Jesus to cherish us. You might struggle under decades of debris and chicken poop until you start to believe you will never rise above it. Then Jesus reaches out His hand and calls you a rare treasure. "But God demonstrates his own love for us in this: While we were still sinners, Christ died for us" (Romans 5:8).

Jesus sees our potential. He has the desire, knowledge, and power to help us become all He created us to be. We can be "confident of this, that he who began a good work in you will carry it on to completion until the day of Christ Jesus" (Philippians 1:6).

Restoring vintage cars requires countless hours of hard, dirty work. Each piece must be examined. Some parts are replaced while others involve modification or perhaps refinishing. Those who have restored a vehicle often say that they know every nut and bolt, every nook and cranny personally.

When we accept Jesus into our heart, He gives us the courage to examine our life with new purpose and insight. He helps us replace bad habits for God-honoring ones. Like David, we can invite God to examine our hearts. "Search me, God, and know my heart; test me and know my anxious thoughts. See if there is any offensive way in me, and lead me in the way everlasting" (Psalm 139:23–24).

Inviting God to examine our heart can be unnerving. Yet, as we allow God access to the inner places of our heart, we experience a desire to purify our thoughts that only God

*Restoration
always costs.*

can provide. God promises in Ezekiel 11:19, "I will give them an undivided heart and put a new spirit in them; I will remove from them their heart of stone and give them a heart of flesh."

Even when this is our desire, it is not something we can do. Restoration is from the inside out. Spraying a fresh coat of paint will cover rust for a while, but it always resurfaces. Rust, like the effects of sin, must be removed before it is primed and repainted. Only God can reverse sin-rust. Only God can give us a new heart.

Restoration always costs. Street rod enthusiasts rarely speak of monetary costs. Nicked knuckles testify to countless hours of hard work plus lots of blood, sweat, and gears. There is not a square inch that has not known the touch of their hand intimately because without this intimate encounter, restoration could not happen.

> Never fear how intimately Jesus knows you. Fear if He did not.

God knows us. He knows when we sit and when we stand. Before a word is on our tongue, he knows it completely (Psalm 139:2–4). Never fear how intimately Jesus knows you. Fear if He did not. Jesus knows every nook and cranny of our hearts. That would be intimidating if He was not fully committed to our restoration. "And the God of all grace . . . will himself restore you and make you strong, firm and steadfast" (1 Peter 5:10).

It was not a bolt that nicked Jesus' knuckle. It was a nail that pierced His hands and feet. Yet, the writer of Hebrews revealed that it was "For the joy set before him he endured the cross, scorning its shame, and sat down at the right hand of the throne of God" (Hebrews 12:2). That joy was our lives restored. Restoration always costs. But thankfully, Jesus boldly and joyfully proclaims you are worth it.

Restored street rods can hold their hoods up and be proud. What was once a pile of rusty junk buried under decades of debris, is now shiny and new, often better than the original. When God restores our soul, we have a fresh outlook on life. We are the same person, yet everything is changed. "Therefore, if anyone is in Christ, the new creation has come: The old has gone, the new is here!" (2 Corinthians 5:17).

With renewed faith, new hope, new life, we shine with a new heart wholly devoted to our awesome God. But maybe the most amazing thing of all is that when God looks at us, He smiles and says, "Oh yeah, you are totally worth it." Hallelujah! Praise the Lord.

Do not store up for yourselves treasures on earth, where moths and vermin destroy, and where thieves break in and steal. But store up for yourselves treasures in heaven, where moths and vermin do not destroy, and where thieves do not break in and steal. For where your treasure is, there your heart will be also.

—Matthew 6:19–20

Listen

Read 1 John 1:9

Your sin is not a surprise to God. His forgiveness should not be a surprise to you.

† What rust or dents has God already restored? What is He working on?

† Walk this day through God's body shop. Do you hear the hammer and chisel? Smell the fresh paint? See the box of new parts? Does your horn work?

† Journal this day's restoration. Ask for patience or courage. Express hope-filled gratitude whether you are still hooked up to the tow truck or ready to roll.

At the Cross

The cross. The nails. The shame.
All of my sin. All of the blame.
God could have done something
To stop the pain and the suffering.

Why did He not put an end
To that awful humiliation?
How much did He expect Jesus to bear?
Oh, how I wish I could have been there.

I know exactly what I would have done
If that had been my beloved son!
I would have taken those nails, bent them in half.
Those people, those soldiers, they would not dare laugh.

I'd twist those cruel nails till they were useless.
Until their awful sting was rendered painless.
There was no need for the hammer and nails,
His love held Him there. And His love never fails.

I know this for sure, but I was not there.
Now centuries later at the same cross I stare.
The nails did not cause the pain on His face.
It was taking the sin of the whole human race.

And when He cried, "Why have You forsaken Me?"
I know it was to His Father, but did He ask it of me?
Did He see in that instant?
Although He was innocent

The fate of those who would reject Him
And remain condemned in their sin?
As if for the first time, I face Calvary.
I see what I did; and what He did for me.

The soldiers used nails to pierce Holy flesh,
But God's plan was perfect, I now can attest.
The nails did not hold His feet and His hands.
What nail could ever hold the Great I Am?

What God nailed to the cross on that day
Is still there today. And always will stay.
So, when we hear the trumpet's final blast,
We need not worry when we breathe our last.

For there, upon that cross we will still see
Our sin nailed there for all eternity.
What was meant for evil, God meant for good.
God's love revealed with nails and wood.

Listen

Read Hebrews 12:2

Take a cross, picture of a cross, nail, or piece of wood to hold in your hand as you re-read the poem, aloud if you can. Pause for a moment and fix your eyes on the cross.

† What thought, word, phrase, or mental picture has God imprinted upon your heart?

† Write down your initial thoughts and/or feelings.

† As your day resumes, let the cross permeate your thoughts and your perception.

† Journal the insights God has revealed about Himself and about you.

LISTEN FOR HIS VOICE

Epilogue

*Teach me your way, Lord, that I may rely on
your faithfulness; give me an undivided heart,
that I may fear your name.*

—Psalm 86:11

I sincerely hope these devotions have deepened your love and appreciation for the awesome God we serve. You might wonder if the ears of my heart have always been trained to listen for God's voice. The answer is no. I had set aside time to read my Bible and pray. I memorized Scripture. I listened to Christian radio and podcasts. I attended weekly services and Bible study. All these things were good and beneficial. But what I desperately needed was some dew-soaked fleece, some tangible connection. The realization that I could not fulfill my need was the beginning of my training. "The fear of the Lord is the beginning of wisdom, And the knowledge of the Holy One is understanding" (Proverbs 9:10 NKJV).

> *The "I" in all I was doing needed to submit to what God wanted to accomplish in me.*

Training, whether a dog, horse, grapevine, Bonsai tree, athlete, or child, is a process whereby someone with greater knowledge guides the subject to achieve a level of excellence not possible on their or its own. Frustration would ensue until my heart's ear was trained to listen for His voice. The "I" in all I was doing needed to submit to what God wanted to accomplish in me. Sometimes, like in "Smitten by Mittens," the experience feels surreal, yet the truth is startling. God has ministered to me during times of deep pain and frustration as well as through the wonders of nature. Still, as a strong-willed child, I often insist on doing things my way. The devotion "Rust to Restoration" is the product of one such power struggle.

It was the final morning of a three-day retreat. The announcement of a special guest speaker at lunch intrigued us. The instructions were simple: bring your Bible and a pen. Lunch would be provided along with speaker notes.

We chatted excitedly with our chosen table mates. Anticipation grew as we wondered who the nationally renowned speaker would be. No one was prepared for the next announcement. Each of us was to pick up a boxed lunch, beverage, and the pamphlet of speaker notes that was totally blank. We were instructed to find a secluded spot on the grounds and have lunch with Jesus. Alone. "Meditate on Psalm 23 for one hour. Write down whatever thoughts Jesus brings to mind."

I was stunned. One hour? On Psalm 23? Those six verses were committed to memory back in fifth grade. I had recited them countless times. Familiarity suffocated any hope to glean fresh insights during the next sixty minutes.

> *Familiarity suffocated any hope to glean fresh insights during the next sixty minutes.*

But it was a most splendid day. Cheered by a chorus of birds, I quickly found a large smooth rock near a bed of flowers. I read Psalm 23 as slowly as I could, which took just over sixty seconds. No great words of wisdom jumped from the page. I prayed. Maybe God would lead me to a different passage. But no redemptive intervention came.

I listened. Birds sang as the wind rustled through the leaves. The buzz of bees harvesting nectar blended with a dog's distant playful bark. Maybe I was simply supposed to enjoy the day with a grateful heart. "Thank You, Lord of Creation, for this amazingly glorious day. Thank you for the sounds, smells, colors, and the sun's warmth. Thank you for the gift of time to savor Your creation."

Then I began Psalm 23 again. Verse one, as if for the first time. I never got past the third verse that day. "He restores my soul." The words resounded in my head as a rusty old Model A Ford, buried under decades of neglect and chicken poop rumbled up from my heart. The mental image startled me as I began to write. Words flowed onto the pages until the chimes signaled our time was up. With tear-filled eyes, I clutched my Bible more aware than ever before how much my Lord loved me. "He lifted me out of the slimy pit, out of the mud and mire; he set my feet on a rock and gave me a firm place to stand" (Psalm 40:2).

God has trained my heart to listen for His voice. But unless I am intentional about listening for His voice, those ear muscles weaken. Daily time in the Word provides a nutritious spiritual snack. Only time with our Lord keeps our ears tuned to His voice. One thing that works for me is to schedule a lunch date with Jesus a couple of times each month. To avoid appearing pious, I decline other invitations by saying, "That sounds great, but I am having lunch with a friend." After all, it is the truth. I have a lunch date with my friend, Jesus.

> But unless I am intentional about listening for His voice, those ear muscles weaken.

I challenge you to invest an hour in a secluded place or busy café to meditate on a handful of verses as if for the first time. Let Jesus love you as only He can. Protect and treasure these lunch dates. We need never to fear how intimately Jesus knows us in our rust, neglect, and chicken poop. Fear instead what would happen if He did not possess the power and desire to bring us from rust to restoration.

Listen for His voice in the everyday of every day. Allow our Lord to restore your soul as only He can. Awaken fresh appreciation for our Creator so that within your busyness, you can experience a joy beyond measure.

My Dear Reader,

When you want an intimate conversation with your friend, do you choose a venue where the music is so loud you must shout to be heard? Neither do I. Neither does God.

While I enjoy podcasts and music, I purposely disconnect from the noise while in my garden or on walks with my dog. Sometimes, I shut the noise off while driving or sitting at my desk. My listening improves when I give God my full attention.

I strongly encourage limiting electronic versions of the Bible. My leather-covered Bible holds me accountable. When used daily, the oil in my hands conditions the leather as the words on its pages condition my soul.

I hope our precious time together has deepened your love and appreciation for our Lord and Savior. Has God awakened a longing in your heart to listen for His voice? I would love to hear your journey with our Lord. I do not think the angels should have all the fun. Please email me at marietpalecek@gmail. com or visit my website at www.marietpalecek.com. Until next time, listen for His voice in the everyday of every day.

Sincerely,
Marie T. Palecek

Listen

Read Psalm 23 – prayerfully, slowly, as if for the first time

✝ Plan at least an hour without electronics and distractions.

✝ It is just You-and-me,-Lord time. Journal whatever God speaks to you.

✝ Sometimes it helps to close your eyes until your mind clears. Listen for His whisper. Feel His presence. Embrace His love. I often pray, "Speak Lord, Your servant is listening. Fill me with the joy of Your Presence."

LISTEN FOR HIS VOICE

Listen for More

I pray that your love will overflow more and more, and that you will keep on growing in knowledge and understanding.

—Philippians 1:9 (NLT)

It all began with the skunk. Seriously. I envisioned my panicked reader with a skunked-dog emergency frantically trying to remember which devotion had a remedy. Well, it is right here in the back of the book. The skunk remedy was quickly joined by recipes for homemade clay. This section has interesting, but unnecessary information pertaining to some of the devotions. It is here for your *listening* pleasure.

Two Recipes for Homemade Clay-Dough for Molding

Homemade Clay-Dough— Using Baking Soda and Corn Starch*

In a saucepan combine:

- † 2 cups baking soda
- † 1 cup corn starch

Stir until well mixed. Add:

- † 1¼ cups cold water.
- † food coloring, if desired.

Cook over medium heat 10–15 minutes, stirring constantly until thickened.

The mixture should be the consistency of mashed potatoes.

Remove from heat. Dump clay into a bowl and cover with a damp cloth.

When cool to the touch, knead until smooth, and let the creating begin!

This clay can be reused for up to a week if stored in a refrigerator between creations.

Projects can be left out to dry naturally (usually takes twenty-four hours) or can be dried in the oven at a low temperature.

Once dried, creations are not waterproof but useful for paper-clips and such.

Note: This clay is made from natural ingredients, but it is not edible.

Homemade Clay-Dough— Using Flour, Cream of Tartar, and Oil*

Combine in a small bowl and set aside:

+ 1 cup flour
+ 2 teaspoons cream of tartar
+ ½ cup salt

Mix in saucepan (in order):

+ 1 cup water
+ Food coloring
+ 1 Tablespoon vegetable oil

Add dry ingredients to liquid and mix well.

Cook over low to medium heat until dough starts to form.

Dough is fully cooked when it forms a ball.

Remove from heat. Dump into a bowl to cool.

Once cool enough to touch, knead dough for 3–6 minutes until soft.

If dough seems dry, rub hands with oil, then knead dough until soft and pliable.

Store covered.

Creations can be left out for 24–48 hours to harden.

Or dry them in an oven using low temperature.

Creations are not waterproof but can be used for paperclips and such.

Dough can usually be rejuvenated a few times. Rub hands with oil, then knead dough until soft and pliable again.

Note: Although not toxic, dough is not edible.

Easy, Basic Home-Baked Bread (Makes 2 loaves)

Ingredients:

- ✝ 2 envelopes active dry yeast
- ✝ 2 cups warm water
- ✝ ½ cup granulated sugar
- ✝ ½ cup vegetable oil, olive oil, or melted butter
- ✝ 1½ teaspoons salt
- ✝ 2 large eggs
- ✝ 6 cups flour, plus more if needed

1. Dissolve 2 envelopes of active dry yeast in a large bowl with 2 cups warm water, let sit for five minutes. Add the sugar, oil, salt, and beat in eggs until smooth. Add 4 cups flour. Mix well. Add additional flour, ½ cup at a time until dough is firm and releases from sides of bowl. (This usually requires 2–3 cups). Bread making is an art. It is hard to judge the dough at first.

2. Generously flour the surface for kneading. Turn dough onto a floured surface. Knead dough until smooth and elastic, about 6–9 minutes. Place dough in a large, greased bowl. Turn once so top is greased. Cover with dry cloth. Place dough in a warm area, protected from drafts and sunlight. Let rise until doubled in size, about one hour. (This is called proofing).

3. Punch down dough. Turn onto floured surface. Knead about 4–5 minutes. Put back in grease bowl, turning once.

Let rise again, covered, in warm, protected area until almost doubled. About 45 minutes.

4. Punch down dough again. Turn onto floured surface. Knead 1–3 minutes. Divide dough in half. Shape into two loaves. Place loaves in two greased 9x5-inch loaf pans. Cover loaves and let rise in a warm, protected area until double in size. About 45–60 minutes.

5. Bake at 350° for 30–35 minutes or until golden brown. Remove bread from pans to cool. Or better yet, savor fresh baked bread while it is still warm and the butter disappears into it immediately.

Wonderfully Made
For Healing

Do you know that you are "fearfully and wonderfully made"? (Psalm 139:14). The Hebrew word *yare* is translated here as "fearfully." Yare means to revere, to stand in awe of, or to fear. It is the same root word used in Proverbs 1:7 which says, "The fear of the Lord is the beginning of knowledge." When we begin to understand how awesome God is, we revere Him. We stand in awe. When we begin to understand how awesomely God created each of us, we should likewise stand in awe. Not in how awesome *we* are, but how awesome our Creator is to have created us with such detail.

God created our body to heal itself. A simple cut on the finger triggers your body's defense system to respond to an injury and begin the healing process almost immediately. Coagulants are rushed to clog the blood flow. The extra blood in the area assists in regenerating skin tissue to fill in the gap caused by the cut. You can learn how to apply a butterfly bandage and include butterfly strips in your first aid kit to aid your body's ability to heal quickly and efficiently.

Have your fingers ever gotten too close to the chopping knife? Do you know anyone who lost the tip of their toe? Amazingly, our body often regenerates skin tissue across these areas without forming the normal scar tissue. Most of the time, nerve endings are also regenerated. In some cases, although not common, an entire tip has regenerated itself. Doctors are baffled as to why regenerated fingertips usually lack a fingerprint, whereas regenerated toes retain that ability. Sometimes, a fingernail or toenail will regenerate itself with a new nail. Other times the body regenerates scar tissue over the area. The success or failure of regenerated fingertips, toes, or nails is inconsistent. Sometimes it happens. Sometimes not.

How to De-Skunk Your Dog

In my opinion, God went a little overboard on this defensive weapon. The persistent oily spray bonds to your dog's fur and skin as it releases oily droplets into the air. You should keep your dog outside. Those airborne oil droplets will adhere to surfaces in your home. I also highly recommend that you wear several layers of disposable gloves and old clothes that you can throw away. So far, only two of my dogs encountered these darling little creatures.

Skunk spray stings the eyes. The eyes are almost always included in the primary target. Use eye drops or water to rinse the eyes. Be careful not to use too much pressure. Avoid getting any of the solutions below in your dog's eyes.

Solution #1

Tomato juice.

This age-old remedy certainly helps. Rinse your dog. Coat their body with tomato juice, and massage it into their skin. Avoid the eyes. Wait twenty to thirty minutes. Rinse and shampoo. Repeat once or twice. I have not found this solution to be very efficient, but it helps.

Solution #2

Hydrogen peroxide, baking soda, Dawn® dishwashing liquid, apple cider vinegar, dog shampoo.

Step One: Rinse dog with water.

Step Two: Mix one cup hydrogen peroxide with a quarter cup baking soda and a teaspoon of Dawn® dishwashing liquid. Double or triple mixture depending on your dog's size. Apply solution to your dog's coat, making sure to get to the skin, but avoid the eyes. Let soak for no longer than twenty minutes. Rinse and shampoo with dog shampoo.

Step Three: Mix a solution of one part apple cider vinegar with two parts water. Pour solution over dog's coat. Make sure it gets to the skin. Avoid the eyes. Let soak for five to ten minutes. Rinse and shampoo with dog shampoo.

Repeat if necessary.

Solution #3

Nature's Miracle Skunk Odor Remover (http://www.naturesmiracle.com/):

I have heard this stuff really works. If you have hunting dogs, live in the country, or just enjoy the outdoors with your dog, maybe keep some on hand.

Solution #4

Professional groomer.

Ask first. Do not assume they can or want to handle the task. Transporting your dog with its airborne oil droplets in your vehicle is another subject.

Waterproof, Wind-Resistant Fire Starters

Materials needed:

- † Combustible containers
- † Combustible materials
- † Wax
- † An old pan to melt wax
- † Stick for stirring
- † Combustible containers include cardboard egg cartons (not plastic or Styrofoam) that are separated before or after you add wax. Or you can use small paper drinking cups (not plastic or Styrofoam).
- † Combustible materials include wood shavings, dryer lint, and/or newspapers.
- † My preference is clean, dry, untreated wood shavings/ mulch.
- † For the wax, collect old candles, used wax from wax-warmers, or purchase paraffin wax in canning or craft supplies.
- † You will need a clean, old pot to melt the wax that is no longer used for food.
- † Tin soup cans are not advisable for safety reasons.
- † For a stirring stick, you can use a chopstick, paint stir stick, dowel rod, or a retired spatula or spoon.

Instructions:

1. Lay out containers on a surface that won't be "upset" about wax over-flowage. Keep in mind that you want the wax to overflow and seep through the containers. Cover your table with several layers of cardboard, plastic, or use a piece of scrap lumber. Cooled wax can be scraped from most smooth surfaces.

2. Fill containers with combustible materials. Press materials into wells, firm but with enough space for wax to flow around materials. Overfilling is fine, just seal with wax.

3. Melt wax in pot, stirring as needed. Keep in mind that wax is flammable.

4. A water bath is recommended, although not necessary.

5. Slowly, pour hot melted wax over combustible materials in containers.

6. Let cool a bit, then pour more wax so that the combustible materials are coated with wax.

7. Once cooled, store in container or zip lock bags for easy transportation.

8. If using egg cartons, separate before or after filling. If afterwards, use tin snip or scissors to separate.

Note: I prefer egg cartons since it is easier to light a corner with a match.

Broken Communion

Prepare a piece of bread, dinner roll, or cracker. Plus, pour some wine, grape juice, or water.

Break the bread or cracker. It is interesting to remember that grapes must be broken to make the wine or juice. If you use water, let it become for you Living Water (John 7:38).

Note: this type of "communion" is a prayer. The elements do not change into the body and blood of Christ. This prayer simply celebrates your "common union" with Jesus, who was broken for you and understands your brokenness. Nothing more. Nothing less.

We do not always recognize encounters with God. In Exodus 3:5, Moses was clueless when God told him, "Take off your sandals, for the place where you are standing is holy ground." Genesis 28:10–19 describes Jacob's encounter with the Lord in a dream. "When Jacob awoke from his sleep, he thought, 'Surely the Lord is in this place, and I was not aware of it.'" In Luke 24:13–35, two disciples walked with Jesus from Jerusalem to Emmaus. That is only seven miles. The average walking pace is 2 miles per hour. So, they walked and talked for about four or five hours. Can you imagine walking with Jesus for seven miles and remaining clueless as to who He was? Verse 31 says their eyes were not opened until Jesus broke the bread.

Sometimes our brokenness blinds us and prevents us from realizing that Jesus is with us. Sometimes, it is our brokenness that opens our eyes to recognize His presence. Let the elements of broken bread and wine open your eyes. Invite Jesus to reveal Himself to you, whether through your brokenness or through His.

Jesus invites you into His brokenness. "The Lord Jesus on the same night in which He was betrayed took bread; and when He had given thanks, He broke it and said, 'Take, eat; this is

My body which is broken for you; do this in remembrance of Me'" (1 Corinthians 11:23–24 NKJV).

Pray either before or after you take the elements of brokenness. You can pray from your heart or use the prayer below. There is no right or wrong way to do this. This is between you and the Lord. And He is overjoyed to be with you right now, at this moment. Can you feel His embrace? His Presence? He is not in the bread or wine; He is in you. "Do you not realize that Christ Jesus is in you?" (2 Corinthians 13:5). Celebrate your union with Jesus.

Prayer

Lord, thank you for the privilege of sharing Your brokenness with You. Thank you, also, for Your Presence in my brokenness. Remind me through the elements of bread and wine of Your willingness to be broken for me. To be broken because of my sin. To be broken so that I can be whole and holy. Help me be aware of Your Holy Spirit dwelling within me so that my thoughts, words, and actions can bring You glory. Lord Jesus, fill me with joy in Your Presence. Fill me with Your Spirit. Let me rejoice and rest in You. In Jesus' precious name. Amen.

Listen
Read 1 Corinthians 11:23–24

If you chose to journal, date your entry. Include a note of this season of your life.

† What has Jesus revealed to you about your brokenness? Or your blessings?

† What has Jesus revealed about His brokenness? His love? Himself?

† What have you laid down before the Lord this day? Is it broken or restored? Is your heart broken, rejoicing, or trembling? Are you dealing with doubt, fear, or uncertainty? Are you filled with faith, knowledge, or assurance?

† Just let the words flow. Do not worry whether they make any sense. This is just between you and the Lord. No worries. The Lord is with you. Jesus' last words in Matthew's Gospel are "And be sure of this: I am with you always, even to the end of the age" (Matthew 28:20 NLT).

Notes

Prologue

For further study, here are the locations of the different Bible events I mentioned in this devotional:

Sitting at Jesus' feet	See Luke 8:35; 10:39
Flaming Bushes	See Exodus 3
Dew-Soaked Fleece	See Judges 6
Evening in Garden	See Genesis 3:8
Jesus on beach	See Mark 4
Jesus on hillside	See Matthew 5
God is the same	See Hebrews 13:8
Talking Donkeys	See Numbers 22; 2 Peter 2
Whisper from cliff	See Exodus 33; 1 Kings 19
Pillar of Fire	See Exodus 13

Imagine

1. Merriam-Webster.com Dictionary, Merriam-Webster, https://www.merriam-webster.com/dictionary/imagination. Accessed 15 Apr. 2021.

2. https://www.honeybeesuite.com Honey Bee Suite: A Better Way to Bee

To Know Her is to Love Her

1. "To know her is to love her" is a commonly misquoted phrase from an English poet named Samuel Rogers (July 30, 1763–December 18, 1855). His original quote was "To know her was to love her." Several songs have used versions of the misquote including, Phil Spector, Dolly Parton, Linda Ronstadt, Emmylou Harris, Bobby Vinton, and The Beatles.

The Nudge

1. MercyMe, "I Can Only Imagine," *The Very Best of MercyMe*, Columbia Records Group, 2018

The Green Football

1. Chris Tomlin, "We Fall Down." https://www.youtube.com/watch?v=7Ge9O_HOKcE

Smitten by Mittens

1. For more information about Hemingway's polydactyl cats, visit the Ernest Hemingway Home and Museum website: https://www.hemingwayhome.com/our-cats

2. https://PresidentialPetsMuseum.com/Theodore-Rossevelts-Slippers/

In Lieu of

1. "O, Be Careful," Copyright © 1956 by Zondervan Music Publishers https://hymnary.org/text/o_be_careful_little_eyes_what_you_see#tune

2. Handford, Martin. *Where's Waldo?*, Somerville, MA: Candlewick, 1997.

Pearly Wisdom

1. https://www.thepearlsource.com/facts-about-pearls/how-pearls-are-made.php

Lost. Found. Home.

1. https://thoughtcatalog.com/katee-fletcher/2020/09/will-rogers-quotes/
2. Cory Asbury, "Reckless Love", *Heaven Come 2017* https://www.youtube.com/watch?v=6xx0d3R2LoU

Salvation's Chrysalis

1. https://animals.howstuffworks.com/insects/caterpillar3.htm

Broken

1. Alcoholics Anonymous https://www.aa.org

If you, or a loved one, are struggling with an addiction, get support. Search for programs through your local church or find local charters. Here are some websites that might help:

National Institute on Alcohol Abuse and Alcoholism, https://www.niaaa.nih.gov

Christian Counseling for Sex and Porn Addiction, https://faithfulandtrue.com

Narcotics Anonymous World Services, https://www.na.org

2. The quote, "I know not what the future holds, but I know who holds the future" is attributed to Homer. There are many variations of this quote. It did not originate with me.

Acknowledgements

To Him who is able to do immeasurably more than all
we ask or imagine, according to His power that is at
work in us, to Him be the glory!
—*Ephesians 3:20–21*

First and foremost, I acknowledge my Lord and Savior for doing immeasurably more than I could ever ask or imagine. To Him be all the glory. I never cease to be amazed by what He can accomplish in us and through us. Ultimately, whatever good we might achieve on this earth is His fulfillment of the Philippians 1:6 promise that "He who began a good work in you will carry it on to completion." That reality keeps pride at bay and permits me to stand in awe even when the work of His hands comes through mine. So, "to Him who is able," I rightly give all glory, honor, praise, and immense gratitude for the privilege of sharing His love. Permit me to introduce you to a few of the instruments God has used to support, encourage, and challenge me:

John E. Palecek: For better or worse, through almost five decades, my husband has been at my side and in my face. As God ordained, two become one, so we share our accomplishments as well as our shortfalls. I have depended on his support and encouragement to spur me through times of doubt as well as moments of inspiration. His servant's heart cheerfully understands my need for solitude in the Lord's presence. His love and unfailing commitment to our marriage continues to challenge me to be a better person.

Peter Palecek: After twenty brutal years of infertility, the birth of our son, Peter, was truly a most grateful blessing. Peter means "rock." My son's rock-solid faith, courage, and character inspire me each day. He is indeed "fearfully and wonderfully made!" To say I am proud would be a gross understatement. I pray daily for him to continue to grow in wisdom and stature and in favor with God and men (Luke 2:52). I pray that he stays true to what God has entrusted to him, firm in his faith, and living Proverbs 3:5–6 each day.

Carol Thill: It never ceases to amaze me how God orchestrates seemingly random people and events to fulfill His ultimate plan for each of us. No matter how many may follow, there is a place in our hearts reserved for "firsts": first love, first car, first kiss, and first loss. "First light" holds a special place of honor reserved for a specific person or event God has used to open your heart, eyes, and mind to the wonder-filled truth of His Word. For me that person is Carol. Her steadfast faith awakened within me the desire to experience my Lord and Savior through a personal relationship in lieu of religion. Carol's wisdom, discernment, and love continues to inspire me. She has challenged and affirmed my faith for almost four decades. Her introduction to the wonder of God's Word released a cascade of blessings which have enriched my life beyond measure. She is my Romans 13:8 debt which will never be repaid.

Beth L. Dutton: Few people are blessed with a soul sister who is a constant source of inspiration and comfort. With Beth, I am free to think aloud. I cherish her wisdom and faith as a dear friend and faithful writing partner. Her touch upon my heart and this book are treasures beyond earthly value. Her encouragement, challenges, and expertise grace each page. From chats and emails in the middle of the night, to refreshing breakfasts at Perkins, much of who I am, I owe to our friendship. Gratefully, she is also a Romans 13:8 debt and a treasured friend.

Mary Anne Juola-Rausch: When you met my mom in the devotion called "To Know Her Is To Love Her," you might have missed the inspiration she was throughout my life. Through triumphs and defeats, she refused to allow her struggle with alcohol and drug addiction to define who she was: a beloved child of God. Her passion for writing is in my DNA. Her faith remained strong when everything else threatened to pull her down. Our friendship was truly an answer to prayer. During the decades of turbulence, I honestly feared relief would be my only sentiment upon her passing. But God is good. I am forever grateful for the gift of heartache as I embrace the aching void her triumphant entry into heaven has left in my heart. I miss her. I truly do. She was a friend like no other.

William C. Rausch: Every child needs someone who believes in them. I grew up as the "apple" of my father's eye. That equipped this strong-willed girl with the determination to become the person he always believed I was. His foresight a few years before his untimely death was a greater gift to me than either of us could have known. Instinctively, he recognized the searching ache in my heart, even if he did not understand it. Relying solely on the advice of "the nice lady at the bookstore," he chose the Bible that totally changed my life. That step out of his comfort zone gave me the Words of Life that have brought so much comfort. Joyfully, I read God's Word each day as a gift from both my earthly father and my Heavenly Father. No matter my age, I will always be Daddy's little girl.

Four-legged mentors: This book would not be possible without the many life lessons from my beloved pets. It has been an honor and humbling experience to learn from the dogs and cats who have shared our home, travels, and heart. All were rescues. Some with years of abuse which compromised their willingness to trust. Through their unique personalities and diverse backgrounds, each taught me how to love and serve my Lord so that I can live Deuteronomy 6:5 more fully "Love the Lord your God with all your heart and with all your soul and with all your strength." Visit my website at www.marietpalecek.com to see their faces and hear more of their story.

Canine mentors: Lady, our regal Australian shepherd mix whom you met in "Abiding Leash." Mindy, our uniquely playful Samoyed malamute mix. Jake, our Shepherd mix with a gentle brute strength. Gus, our border collie terrier mix who loved everyone, maybe a little too much. Chopper, our comical German shepherd rescue dog who redefined trust and loyalty ("Green Football"). Dixie, an Aussie mix, is our latest rescue. Look for her charming character in future books.

Feline mentors: As a tiny kitten, Stacy was adopted by three canine siblings. Later, he adopted Gus, plus entertained several strays until we found them forever homes. Denali reigned as feline queen for fifteen years. She adored her canine buddy, Gus, who was as smitten by her as we were. You met her in "Smitten by Mittens" and "Spiritual Whiskers."

Jenny Kochert and Mindy Kiker of FlourishWriters: Without the encouragement, guidance, coaching, and knowledge of Jenny and Mindy, this book would still be in my dream bucket. Thankfully, God provides. Joining FlourishWriters Academy was an investment in sharpening my writing skills, goal setting, achieving, and filling my knowledge gap with wisdom. These two ladies have the gift of mentoring each writer as if they were the only student on the roster. You do not feel like you are eating from the basket of loaves and fishes being passed around the hill. You are personally served and acknowledged.

Gleniece Lytle: Have you ever looked at the backside of a tapestry or work of embroidery? It is a mess. Globs of thread and knots intertwine with each other with no visible plan or pattern. That is how my life felt. Through journaling, God revealed the flip side of my tapestry and the breathtaking picture of His Romans 8:28 plan for my life. My editor, Gleniece, took that tapestry, trimmed the jagged edges, and framed it so that it could be shared with you, my readers. I cannot imagine this book without her touch, edits, encouragement, and instruction.

Nelly Murariu: From the cover to the interior design, Nelly masterfully embellished the words inscribed on these pages into a work of art. I pray that her creative handiwork will minister to you, my dear reader, as much as the words printed on these pages. And when the butterflies take your heart and mind from the pages, it is not a distraction. It is an invitation to go on an adventure with our Lord. So, Listen for His voice and enjoy the journey.

Finally, my thanks to you, my readers. Ultimately, without you these words would simply be journal entries. I cannot shake the conviction that these humble insights, which originate from God's Word, are not for my sole benefit. They are to be presented to you for His glory. May they inspire you so that God can touch your heart as only He can. I pray that you will never settle to simply enjoy life. Instead, listen for His voice each day. Embrace the abundant life God has prepared for you—life to the fullest (John 10:10).

About the Author

Marie T. Palecek is passionate to discover God in the simple things of life and share those morsels with dear readers. In her creative Scripture-inspired devotions, you'll encounter humor, trivia, and personal challenges. She takes readers on a journey to uncover how deep and wide God's love is for them, praying they deepen their connection with God.

Marie lives in Minnesota with John, her husband of almost fifty years. During twenty years of infertility, God nurtured her faith before their son, Peter, arrived. They have shared their home with numerous rescue dogs and felines who show up in the pages of her books. She is training her latest rescue, Dixie, as a certified therapy dog. When not at the keyboard, Marie enjoys crocheting, scrapbooking, gardening, camping, fishing, and snowmobiling.